D0058393

CONSISTENTLY OPPOSING KILLING

From Abortion to Assisted Suicide, the Death Penalty, and War

Edited by Rachel M. MacNair and Stephen Zunes

Westport, Connecticut
London

Library of Congress Cataloging-in-Publication Data

Consistently opposing killing : from abortion to assisted suicide, the death penalty, and war / edited by Rachel M. MacNair and Stephen Zunes.
p. cm.
Includes bibliographical references and index.
ISBN-13: 978–0–313–35278–2 (alk. paper)
1. Violence—Moral and ethical aspects. 2. Life and death, Power over. 3. Bioethics. I. MacNair, Rachel. II. Zunes, Stephen.
BJ1459.5.C66 2008
179′.7—dc22 2007050088

British Library Cataloguing in Publication Data is available.

Library of Congress Catalog Card Number: 2007050088
ISBN-13: 978–0–313–35278–2

First published in 2008

Praeger Publishers, 88 Post Road West, Westport, CT 06881
An imprint of Greenwood Publishing Group, Inc.
www.praeger.com

Printed in the United States of America

The paper used in this book complies with the Permanent Paper Standard issued by the National Information Standards Organization (Z39.48–1984).

10 9 8 7 6 5 4 3 2 1

Contents

Introduction: The Power of Being Consistent

Rachel M. MacNair

> *"With consistency, beautiful and undeviating, human life from its commencement to its close, is protected by common law.... By law it is protected not only from immediate destruction, but from every degree of actual violence..."*
>
> —*James Wilson, United States Supreme Court Justice, signer of the Declaration of Independence and the U.S. Constitution, "Lectures on Law,"* 1791

This book expands on the *consistent life ethic,* which has also been called the "seamless garment" approach to issues of socially approved violence. We will be making the case that issues of violence are connected, their solutions are also connected, and there is persuasive power in being consistent by leaving no loopholes in the arguments against violence.

The issues that have been selected by the organization Consistent Life are war, abortion, the death penalty, euthanasia, poverty, and racism. Many other issues could also be included where brevity is unnecessary, and so are included in this book.

Despite constant media misrepresentations or neglect, both the peace movement and the pro-life movement have been strong and have achieved great things. We want to make the case that they could achieve much more in harmony with each other rather than spiraling down into the thoughtless stereotypes so common to politics and the press.

HOW EFFECTIVE HAS THE PEACE MOVEMENT BEEN?

The peace movement has ended already-established wars. As far back as the nineteenth century, the United States war with Mexico ended earlier than President Polk wished and with less than he wished to gain because, despite military success, the opposition was fierce. Some historians argue that the anti-imperialist movement limited the extent of the U.S. conquest of the Philippines in the late 1800s and early 1900s, leading the way to Philippine independence. Pressures from the peace movement may have limited U.S. intervention during the Mexican Revolution in the 1910s and softened later tensions. Historians find that the antiwar movement had an impact on the war policies toward Vietnam of Presidents Johnson and Nixon.[1] They were pushed to de-escalate and finally withdraw. They preferred losing to using tactical nuclear weapons, for fear of public reaction.

How many wars have been contemplated but have got shelved for fear of public reaction? We can never know. Additionally, possible wars have been prevented before they even got to that stage through techniques developed by the peace movement such as conflict resolution skills, international cooperation, treaties, and nonviolent mass movements to resist dictators and unjust policies.

As for the nuclear arms race, let me quote from historian Lawrence S. Wittner:

> There is also considerable evidence that it was the peace movement that brought an end to the Cold War. The peace movement's struggle against the nuclear arms race and its clearest manifestation, nuclear testing, led directly to Kennedy's 1963 American University address and to the Partial Test Ban Treaty of that year, which began Soviet-American détente. The speech was partially written by Norman Cousins, founder and co-chair of the National Committee for a Sane Nuclear Policy, America's largest peace group . . .
>
> When the hawkish Reagan administration revived the Cold War and escalated the nuclear arms race, these actions triggered the greatest outburst of peace movement activism in world history . . . In Europe [and the U.S.], in the fall of 1983 some five million people turned out . . . Reagan was stunned. . . .
>
> Consequently, in January 1984, Reagan delivered a remarkable public address calling for peace with the Soviet Union and for a nuclear-free world . . . But the Soviet leadership was not interested in following up . . . until the advent of Mikhail Gorbachev in March 1985. Gorbachev,

> unlike his predecessors, was ready to take action, for he was a movement convert.
>
> His "New Thinking" . . . was almost a carbon copy of the peace movement's program. As Gorbachev himself declared: "The new thinking took into account and absorbed the conclusions and demands of . . . the movements of physicians, scientists, and ecologists, and of various antiwar organizations." Not surprisingly, then, Reagan and Gorbachev, spurred on by the peace movement, moved rapidly toward nuclear disarmament treaties and an end to the Cold War.[2]

Even more impressive has been the worldwide eruption in using nonviolent tactics and "people power" for opposing colonialism, dictatorships, racism, and stolen elections, along with advancing civil and human rights. Though such nonviolent rebellions have occurred around the world and have occurred throughout history,[3] their use has grown dramatically in recent times. In 1989 alone, unarmed insurrections took place in countries that held 32 percent of the world's population. The twentieth century saw such an outburst that Walter Wink points out that if we added up the populations of all these countries, it would cover about 64 percent of humanity.[4] Nonviolent action has moved from being a fringe idea of eccentric pacifists to becoming something that has worked so often and so well that some promote it not out of principle but for practicality.

The movement against the death penalty is related. Executions used to be widespread, deliberately brutal, and for trivial offenses, so the death penalty abolition movement has made remarkable progress. Capital punishment has been abolished in most countries. Where it is practiced, it is more likely to be hidden from public view rather than on display with a carnival atmosphere, to attempt humane as opposed to tortuous methods, and to be restricted to major offenses. Ending the practice is a realistic possibility within a few generations at the most. The movement has been effective, and bids fair to finish the job.

HOW EFFECTIVE HAS THE PRO-LIFE MOVEMENT BEEN?

While both abortion and euthanasia have been common throughout history, I will focus here on more recent events. When conception was scientifically discovered to be the biological beginning of an individual life in the nineteenth century, there was a remarkably successful campaign in many areas of the world by medical people to push for the abortion prohibition laws that had been at point of "quickening" to apply back to the point of conception. The major challenge to this by eugenicists and the Nazis became discredited, though illegal abortions were prevalent. By the 1960s, a move to legalize abortion arose.

In a major political tsunami, the U.S. Supreme Court handed down its decisions in the *Roe v. Wade* and *Doe v. Bolton* cases on January 22, 1973. Abortion prohibition laws of all fifty states were swept away, and other countries were influenced accordingly. Despite existing before then, the right-to-life movement in the United States generally regards that day as the starting point of its struggle.

How successful has the movement been in the United States? Measuring its success in the narrow terms of being able to overturn *Roe v. Wade* is remarkably inadequate. It would only mean legislation *can* be passed, not that it *will* be. There is also only so much legislation alone can do. But there has been remarkable success in two other areas.

The first area is the impact on the practice of abortion itself. In the United States, the raw numbers, the abortion rate per number of women, and ratio of abortions to live births have all been dropping steadily for several years. The number of abortion clinics in the United States has dropped precipitously, from over 2,000 in 1990 to less than 700 by 2005. Abortion has become more concentrated in these clinics, away from the hospitals, which means that the drop in clinics is indeed a dramatic drop in availability.

Furthermore, the numbers of abortions are being kept up by repeat abortions. The drop in first-time abortions is truly dramatic. Because no one can have a repeat abortion without having a first abortion, and because repeat abortions will stop as women pass reproductive age, an even more dramatic decline can be expected over the next few years.

The stigma on doctors who perform abortions has never entirely disappeared, even among people who support abortion. The idea of increasing the number of abortion providers by qualifying non-doctors to perform them could have a boomerang effect: How many doctors will continue if non-doctors can do it? This would take away the one shred of reputation they have left.

Therefore, the abortion business is currently in a state of deep decline, at least in the United States. The collapse of the business is well underway, and many of the supports necessary to keep it from collapsing further are not in place. Nor is this merely a wishful-thinking bias of opponents. For example, the lead attorney in the *Roe v. Wade* case, Sarah Weddington, said, "When I look back on the decision, I thought these words had been written in granite. But I've learned it was not granite. It was more like sandstone. The immediate problem is, where will the doctors come from?"[5]

This is the view in the United States. The situation varies much more in other countries, with upsurges and subsidings. Poland is a country which had widespread legalized abortion and later banned it. The maternal death rate went down, contrary to the expectations of abortion defenders.[6]

The second area where the right-to-life movement has been remarkably successful is in stopping the slide down the slippery slope. Some predicted that once abortion was legalized, infanticide and euthanasia of the disabled would follow. Attempts occurred in abundance and used *Roe v. Wade* as a precedent. Yet, infanticide is not widespread, and the margins of euthanasia are still being argued in most places. The juggernaut has not picked up steam as much as it surely would have, had there not been an energetic right-to-life movement opposing it.

INCONSISTENCY AS SABOTAGE

Let us set aside the lunatic fringes—the yellers and haters, bombers and shooters—that all large movements have and are damaged by. They are clearly inconsistent with the goals of any movement against violence and accordingly are commonly condemned.

The deeper question is, what has it done to the peace movement to have so many of its members assume that a "pro-choice" stand is part of the program?

The peace movement is losing influence on many people of tender conscience who are concerned about preventing violence against unborn children and believe that such violence also hurts their mothers. How many such people disbelieve our rhetoric of *peace*, when they perceive it as not consistently applied?

The impact of the abortion debate on politics is excruciating to the fragile peace goals. Elections have something called the "pro-life increment," defined as the votes a candidate gains from opposing abortion minus the votes lost. Polls consistently show that it has been an important factor in close races all over the United States since 1980, most commonly around 3–4 percent of the total votes. This factor sometimes helps the candidate who is better on peace and justice issues, such as Governor Robert Casey of Pennsylvania. But it frequently helps the candidate who is worse on such issues from a peace movement point of view.

If we in the peace movement lose our impact on elections, on legislation, and on policy because of defending abortion, is this loss the price we pay for standing up for our principles? Or is it instead a price the victims of war pay?

If abortion also has victims, then squandering our effectiveness in opposing war for its sake becomes a double tragedy.

Conversely, what has it done to the right-to-life movement to have its political fortunes hitched to politicians who promote war and the death penalty and inadequately fund antipoverty programs?

The movement loses influence on many people of tender conscience concerned about preventing violence against, to use a popular slogan of yesteryears, "Children and Other Living Things." When wars come one after another and military expenditures wreak havoc on the needs of the poor, they see it as massive, visible violence. How many such people disbelieve our rhetoric for *life*, when they perceive it as not consistently applied?

As for politics, the single-issue focus has a marvelous effect on getting U.S. candidates to commit to a more principled rather than compromise-oriented stand, a feature the average peace activist could envy. But it also means that for officeholders, one juicy scandal or one unpopular war or one unheeded major hurricane can leave the already shaky and often neglected legislative goals and policies—and the next election—very vulnerable.

COGNITIVE CONSISTENCY

Does the human mind care whether its beliefs are consistent? Oh, yes! This is among the strongest findings in psychology. The mind has a strong drive to see to it that its beliefs, feelings, and actions are consistent.

In the 1950s, psychologist Leo Festinger noticed strange behavior in some people. These people would predict that some major event—massive floods, the end of the world, the Second Coming, a landing of alien ships from outer space, etc.—would take place on a specific date. The date came and went, but nothing happened. The sensible conclusion was that the prediction was wrong. Some people concluded that this was so, but others generated some astounding explanations for why the prediction was correct, but something had *changed*. They would then proselytize about it. These people had given up their jobs and sold their houses and arranged their lives in such a manner that they would be in trouble if the predictions were wrong. Therefore, the predictions were not wrong. They needed to make reality consistent with their behavior, and they needed to convince other people that reality was consistent with their behavior.

Festinger called the state of having ideas and/or actions out of whack with one another "cognitive dissonance." Many experiments throughout decades verified it: The human urge to avoid inconsistency is strong.[7]

There are exceptions—those who score high on the scale measuring Machiavellianism. An amoral, manipulative mind-set is less bothered by mental or behavioral inconsistency, because it consistently does not care about ethics. Interestingly, item 19 on the most commonly used scale to measure Machiavellianism is "People suffering from incurable diseases should have the choice of being put painlessly to death."[8] Based on Niccolo Machiavelli's writings, euthanasia is one item on this widespread scale to measure this way of thinking.

LINKING ISSUES

The peace movement is accustomed to linking issues to peace. Poverty and racism are structural violence; dictatorships and torture are human rights abuses; domestic abuse and rape are misogynist violence; and pollution is environmental violence. "Peace" means avoiding all forms of violence, not just war. The idea of connecting issues will not be startling to the average peace advocate. It comes naturally to us. This is why making such connections hops quickly to the mind of peace advocates who become convinced of the pro-life position.

On the other hand, right-to-lifers are accustomed to being assertively "single issue," even when it really is a package of issues such as abortion, infanticide, and euthanasia, with occasional related issues as current events require. Pro-lifers are also accustomed to attacks on their consistency and to having to deflect such attacks from people who, from their point of view, are inconsistent themselves.

The argument for consistency never works if it is one-sided. The charge that "pro-lifers think life begins at conception and ends at birth" has never made sense since the whole point of opposing abortion is to *not* have life end at birth. Opposition to infanticide and euthanasia also show it as an inept charge. Moreover, the accusation has been made by people challenging others to be consistent in applying a principle across the board, while being blind to how they were not doing so themselves.

Some have exploited the consistent life ethic to make this point: If you are concerned about abortion, why not be consistent by being concerned about all these other things also? Yet, people who work directly on other single issues, such as gun control or efforts to prevent smoking or drunk driving, are not commonly challenged to think that they must work on everything if they are going to work on anything. It simply becomes a way of watering down abortion. Instead of opposing pro-lifers outright by making cogent arguments, it is proclaiming that the issue is too unimportant to bother with.

Actually, several issue combinations commonly include abortion. For example, suppose a pro-lifer says abortion is a family issue, combined with issues to strengthen the family, the rejoinder would be, "Who are you to impose your ideas of family on others?" If a pro-lifer says abortion is a matter of sexual ethics, combined with other issues of sexual morality, the rejoinder would be, "Who are you to impose your ideas of sex on others?" Again, suppose a pro-lifer says abortion is a religious issue, the rejoinder that is most assured to come back would be, "Who are you to impose your religious views on others?"

Now, if the pro-lifer says abortion is an issue of violence, combined with other issues of violence, the rejoinder is much more difficult. How does it look to say people should not impose an opposition to violence? One can insist abortion is not actually violence, but then the argument is framed in the most effective manner. The consistent life ethic, when used by people who actually mean it, does not water down opposition to abortion, but strengthens it. It puts it in the category of violence, where it belongs.

NOTES AND REFERENCES

1. Small, Melvin. 1988. *Johnson, Nixon, and the Doves*. New Brunswick, NJ: Rutgers University Press.
2. Wittner, Lawrence S. January 2006. "Have Peace Activists Ever Stopped a War?" Paper at a forum sponsored by Historians against the War at the annual meeting of the American Historical Association, http://hnn.us/articles/20367.html
3. For an overview, see MacNair, Rachel. 2004. *History Shows: Winning with Nonviolent Action*. Philadelphia, PA: Xlibris.
4. Wink, Walter. 1998. *The Powers That Be: Theology for a New Millennium*. New York: Doubleday, pp. 116–117.
5. Quoted in the *Milwaukee Journal Sentinel*, February 14, 1998.
6. Abortions reported in Poland: in 1990, 59,417; in 1994, only 782. Women's deaths connected with pregnancy: in 1990, 90; in 1994, 57. Infant deaths and total number of births also went down.
7. For extensive discussion of how this insight applies to the current situation on abortion, see Chapters 4, 5, 6, and 17 of Rachel MacNair, *Achieving Peace in the Abortion War*, http://www.fnsa.org/apaw/ch4.html, http://www.fnsa.org/apaw/ch6.html, and http://www.fnsa.org/apaw/ch17.html.
8. Christie, R. and Geis, F. 1970. *Studies in Machiavellianism*. New York: Academic Press; the gender-inclusive language version was found to perform just as well: Zook, A., and Sipps, G. J. 1985. Reliability Data and Sex Differences with a Gender-free Mach IV. *The Journal of Social Psychology, 126*, 131–132.

CONNECTED VIOLENCE

Word Games Take Lives

William Brennan

The following are excerpts from the introduction to the book Dehumanizing the Vulnerable: When Word Games Take Lives, *published by Life Cycle Books. Reprinted by permission of the author and publisher (copyright Life Cycle Books, 1995). The entire book is available from Life Cycle Books at www.lifecyclebooks.com.*

The power of language to color one's view of reality is profound. In many instances, the most significant factor determining how an object will be perceived is not the nature of the object itself, but the words employed to characterize it. Operating through the lenses of contrasting linguistic symbols, two persons looking at the same phenomenon are likely to come up with sharply divergent observations. Words can also act as a force for justice or a weapon of repression, and instrument of enlightenment or a source of darkness.

The annals of inhumanity are replete with an endless litany of disparaging expressions as well as scores of oppressive actions. The demeaning labels manufactured may become so pervasive that they constitute a full-scale *war of words.* Linguistic reduction of victims to an insignificant, despicable, or dangerous level helps stimulate the kind of destructive thinking that leads ultimately to destructive actions. The victims are cast in such a negative or inconsequential light that whatever is done to them, no matter how horrendous, is considered perfectly justifiable.

A universal set of dehumanizing designations keeps recurring whoever the victims and whatever the period of their victimization. Much of this name-calling can be placed under eight categories:

- *deficient human* ("stupid," "defective," "inferior," "potential life," "lives not worth living")
- *less than human* ("subhuman" and "nonhuman")
- *animal* ("beast" and "lower animal")
- *parasitic creature* ("parasite," "vermin," "lice")
- *infectious disease* ("pestilence," "plague," "epidemic," "infection," "contagion")
- *inanimate object* ("thing," "property," "material," "merchandise")
- *waste product* ("trash," "rubbish," "debris," "garbage," "refuse")
- *non-person* (social, psychological, or legal nonexistence).

This classification of linguistic devaluation furnishes a comprehensive framework for exploring the pervasiveness of defamatory rhetoric and its devastating effects on a diverse spectrum of victims. One of the most remarkable features of anti-life rhetoric is the sheer consistency and stability underlying the denigrating concepts that engulf a wide variety of people rendered expendable. While the range of victims has fluctuated down through the years, the semantic assaults against them have remained stubbornly constant.

Any war, whether semantic or otherwise, requires an identifiable enemy upon whom to impose the derogatory labels. At one time or another almost every imaginable racial, ethnic, religious, age, and social group has suffered the consequences of linguistic abuse, ranging from discrimination to outright annihilation.

The victimized groups selected for analysis in this study are among the most extensively oppressed on record: the unborn, the dependent and/or disabled, women, those exterminated in the Nazi Holocaust (primarily Jews, but also Gypsies, Germans with disabilities, Poles, and "asocials"), the targets of Soviet tyranny, African Americans, and Native Americans.

PLAYING WITH WORDS: THE PSYCHOLOGY OF THE BIG LIE

Phillip Knightley, a keen observer of wartime propaganda, emphasized that when war comes the first casualty is the truth.[1] Consequently, a feature common to any war of words against whatever victims is the patent falsehood of the designations concocted... Those who control language control thought, and eventually semantic corruption leads to the adulteration of thought itself.

An editorial appearing in the September 1970 issue of *California Medicine* contains a revealing statement on lying in the service of killing. The editorial proposes a linguistic strategy of *semantic gymnastics*—"avoidance of the scientific fact, which everyone really knows, that human life begins at conception" and separation of "the idea of abortion from the idea of killing"—as essential for obtaining widespread acceptance of not only abortion, but also euthanasia. Further, the article dubs semantic gymnastics "a schizophrenic sort of subterfuge."[2]

Semantic gymnastics is an exceedingly apt term because it connotes the severe twisting and distorting of language necessary to deny fundamental *scientific facts*, which include the facts that human life exists before birth and that abortion kills human lives in the womb. Likening these denials to a "schizophrenic sort of subterfuge" is considered so extreme that they are placed in the same league as a major mental disorder. However, what is admittedly a strategy comparable to pathological lying is actually endorsed as an appropriate way to promote abortion.

Ever since 1970, the policy of semantic gymnastics has been propagated so often and with such fervor that it has become deeply embedded in the public consciousness. What once had been "the scientific fact, which everyone really knows, that human life begins at conception" has been—through countless repetitions—obscured and reduced to the suspect level of an outmoded, sectarian bias. Thanks to the power of "the big lie," no longer does everyone know that human life begins at conception.

The *California Medicine* editorial did not confine its vocabulary of duplicity to aborted humans, but envisioned other victims as well:

> *Medicine's role with respect to changing attitudes toward abortion may well be a prototype of what is to occur.... One may anticipate further development of these roles as the problems of birth control and birth selection are extended inevitably to death selection and death control.*[3]

Therefore, if semantic gymnastics can be used to deny the humanity of the unborn, they can also be employed to deny the humanity of the born. If semantic gymnastics can be invoked to call abortion something other than killing, they can be relied upon to cover up the destructive nature of euthanasia. Helped along by the enormous inroads made by "the big lie" in the promotion of abortion, euthanasia proponents are resorting to the same kind of linguistic distortions to justify getting rid of undesired humans after birth.

PRESTIGIOUS PLAYERS

The extreme lies and deceptions emanating from this deadly serious game of verbal engineering and manipulation take on enhanced credibility when its most influential players are highly regarded individuals. In the early 1970s a distinguished-looking, authoritative-sounding actor was coached to give a lecture on "The Application of Mathematical Game Theory to Physical Education" to groups of professionals and educators. He was billed as Dr. Myron L. Fox of the Albert Einstein University and dressed up with a fictitious but impressive curriculum vitae. Dr. Fox was instructed "to present his topic and conduct his question-and-answer period with an excessive use of double talk, neologisms, non sequiturs, and contradictory statements. All this was to be interspersed with parenthetical humor and meaningless references to unrelated topics." Afterward, questionnaires were administered to evaluate his talk. Some typical responses were as follows:

> *Excellent presentation, enjoyed listening. Has warm manner. Good flow... Lively examples... Extremely articulate... Good analysis of subject... Knowledgeable.*[4]

Moreover, not a single person in the well-educated audiences detected that the authoritative lecturer was a phony!

Prominent personages with impeccable credentials also play an important role in the successful imposition of language intended to denigrate human beings considered discardable. Contrary to popular belief, although despicable language is often primarily associated with crazed individuals or mobs in the streets, it is far more likely to emanate from highly educated, respectable circles. Eminent people throughout history rank among the most steadfast purveyors of demeaning expressions. In *The Republic*, Plato's advocacy of infanticide (book 5) proceeded from a perception of handicapped children as "inferior creatures." Louis Agassiz, founder of the Museum of Natural History at Harvard University and a leading nineteenth-century scientist, called black people a "degraded and degenerate race."[5] One of America's greatest historians, Francis Parkman (1823–93), associated Indians with "leeches" and "contagions."

Such revelations are not intended to detract from the monumental achievements of these individuals, but to show that even *they* became agents of the prevailing rhetoric. In the hands of revered individuals, the degrading concepts were endowed with enormous credibility. This in turn greatly enhanced their acceptance and facilitated the appalling actions taken against those at the receiving end of the disparaging terminology.

The successful waging of semantic warfare on the contemporary unwanted unborn can likewise be largely attributed to the heavy participation of influential and respectable individuals and organizations. The 1970 *California Medicine* editorial advocating a policy of semantic gymnastics to justify the dehumanization and destruction of unborn humans put it this way: "The very considerable semantic gymnastics which are required to rationalize abortion as anything but taking a human life would be ludicrous if they were not often put forth under *socially impeccable auspices* [italics mine]." Nevertheless, the statement continues, "this schizophrenic sort of subterfuge is necessary" to obtain widespread approval of abortion.

In other words, under the ordinary standards of honest discourse it would be ridiculous ("ludicrous") to maintain that the life taken in abortion is something other than human. However, according to one of the sacrosanct tenets of semantic gymnastics, such an outlandish canard ("this schizophrenic sort of subterfuge") is elevated to the status of an incontestable truth when disseminated by prestigious individuals and institutions ("under socially impeccable auspices").

Similarly, the extensive involvement of prominent people and groups is playing a major role in the proliferation of linguistic assaults against vulnerable human lives after birth.

IDEOLOGICAL FOUNDATIONS OF NAME-CALLING

Semantic warfare does not ordinarily burst upon the scene helter-skelter. It is not an accidental, spontaneous, or chaotic episode, but a deliberate and unremitting phenomenon usually undergirded by fully elaborated systems of concepts, beliefs, and myths.

Theoretical support for many past defamatory labels pinned on blacks, Indians, and Jews can be traced back to the work of eighteenth-century anthropologists and naturalists involved in the task of classifying human beings and other creatures in nature. What began as a legitimate attempt to comprehend the great diversity of human and animal life, however, degenerated into the construction of a great "chain of being," an imposing ideological Goliath for ranking the world's races according to a hierarchy of worth.

The dogma of male supremacy—a set of beliefs that maintains men are stronger, smarter, better, and more important than women—has often functioned as a precondition for the torrent of degrading images and despicable actions imposed upon female members of the human race. Although not all violence against women can be attributed to a patriarchal mindset, the ideology of male superiority is so deeply ingrained in numerous societies and cultures that it has had a profound influence on how men view and treat women. Historically and currently, an overwhelming preponderance of violence against women has been male-induced. And many perpetrators believe that their status as males entitles them to exploit the minds and bodies of women in any way they wish.

All of these ideologies, whatever their idealistic and benevolent guises, share an essential ingredient—they are based on an elitist definition of the human race. And it is this deplorable notion that underlies the explosion of derogatory language directed againt vulnerable populations today and in times past. . . .

DEHUMANIZING LANGUAGE AND ITS HUMANIZING CHALLENGERS

Historically, one of the main reasons for the decline in or termination of oppression against various people and groups has been the presence of individuals who, even during periods when the discrediting semantics predominated, refused to accept the prevailing norms of name-calling. The success of any genuine human rights movement rests in large part on the capacity of its proponents to forge positive, personalized, and exalted images of the victims as worthwhile human beings whose oppression can no longer be tolerated. Renaming formerly degraded individuals as legitimate human lives deserving of respect and esteem will not necessarily achieve a major change in their treatment. However, given sufficient societal and institutional support, positive labels—like negative labels—can effect a profound change in how people are perceived and therefore treated.

Two major authorities are usually cited to sustain the positive labels designed to counteract linguistic oppression—the natural and supernatural orders of creation. According to the *natural law perspective,* all of the victims . . . share one thing in common: a human nature readily demonstrated by appeals to reason, logic, common sense, observation, and scientific findings. The intrinsic value of the victims is based on the democratic, egalitarian principle that all human beings deserve equal protection under the law despite their status, condition, or stage of development. The *divine law tradition* endows human nature with the imprint of spirituality. It portrays all human beings—including the most disabled and defenseless—as individuals of inestimable worth since they are made in the image and likeness of God. References to Holy Scripture and other religious sources furnish the basis for proclaiming the sanctity of every human life.

The secular and sacred foundations of terminology intended to offset massive victimization are often kept separate and distinct. Non-believers and individuals who do not wish to impose a religious viewpoint utilize language emphasizing the humanness of the victims. Others prefer to project a more exalted perception by highlighting the divine origin of all human beings. Still others see the human and divine as complementary levels of existence comprising a compelling cornerstone for challenging the dehumanizing rhetoric forged by perpetrators past and present. During the decades preceding the American Civil War many abolitionists invoked both the natural and supernatural law in their efforts to raise public awareness regarding the true nature of black Americans and the unconscionable conditions that slavery imposed upon them. The defenders of other oppressed groups have done and are doing likewise.

A remarkable strain of consistency permeates the language employed to highlight the human and spiritual nature of individuals and groups subjected to massive victimization. The contemporary opponents of abortion and euthanasia rely on the same range of positive expressions to defend the unwanted unborn and born of today that were used to defend Native Americans, African Americans, Soviet people, Jews, women, and other targets of past oppression. Down through the ages and up to the present the advocates of society's most vulnerable groups have thus drawn upon a common core of personalized designations for focusing on the intrinsic value, humanity, and divinity of those being victimized.

NOTES AND REFERENCES

1. Knightley, Phillip. 1975. *The First Casualty: From the Crimea to Vietnam: The War Correspondent as Hero, Propagandist, and Myth Maker.* New York: Harcourt Brace Jovanovich, A Harvest Book.

2. A New Ethic for Medicine and Society. *California Medicine, 113* (September 1970), 68.

3. Ibid.

4. Naftulin, Donald H., John E. Ware, and Frank A. Donnelly. 1973. The Doctor Fox Lecture: A Paradigm of Educational Seduction. *Journal of Medical Education, 48* (July 1973), 630–635.

5. Lure, Edward. 1960. *Louis Agassiz, A Life in Science.* Chicago: University of Chicago Press, p. 257.

The Left Has Betrayed the Sanctity of Life: Consistency Demands Concern for the Unborn

Mary Meehan

A classic. From Mary Meehan, "Abortion: The Left has betrayed the sanctity of life," The Progressive, *September 1980, volume 44(9): 32–34. Reprinted with permission.*

The abortion issue, more than most, illustrates the occasional tendency of the Left to become so enthusiastic over what is called a "reform" that it forgets to think the issue through. It is ironic that so many on the Left have done on abortion what the conservatives and Cold War liberals did on Vietnam: They marched off in the wrong direction, to fight the wrong war, against the wrong people.

Some of us who went through the anti-war struggles of the 1960s and early 1970s are now active in the right-to-life movement. We do not enjoy opposing our old friends on the abortion issue, but we feel that we have no choice. We are moved by what pro-life feminists call the "consistency thing"—the belief that respect for human life demands opposition to abortion, capital punishment, euthanasia, and war. We don't think we have either the luxury or the right to choose some types of killing and say that they are all right, while others are not. A human life is a human life; and if equality means anything, it means that society may not value some human lives over others.

Until the last decade, people on the Left and Right generally agreed on one rule: We all protected the young. This was not merely agreement on an ethical question: It was also an expression of instinct, so deep and ancient that it scarcely required explanation.

Protection of the young included protection of the unborn, for abortion was forbidden by state laws throughout the United States. Those laws reflected an ethical consensus, not based solely on religious tradition but also on scientific evidence that human life begins at conception. The prohibition of abortion in the ancient Hippocratic Oath is well known. Less familiar to many is the Oath of Geneva, formulated by the World Medical Association in 1948, which included these words: "I will maintain the utmost respect for human life from the time of conception." A Declaration of the Rights of the Child, adopted by the United Nations General Assembly in 1959, declared that "the child, by reason of his physical and mental immaturity, needs special safeguards and care, including appropriate legal protection, before as well as after birth."

It is not my purpose to explain why courts and parliaments in many nations rejected this tradition over the past few decades, though I suspect their action was largely a surrender to technical achievement—if such inventions as suction aspirators can be called technical achievements. But it is important to ask why the Left in the United States generally accepted legalized abortion.

One factor was the popular civil-libertarian rationale for freedom of choice in abortion. Many feminists presented it as a right of women to control their own bodies. When the objection was raised that abortion ruins *another person's* body, they responded that a) it is not a body, just a "blob of protoplasm" (thereby displaying ignorance of biology); or b) it is not really a "person" until it is born. When it was suggested that this is a wholly arbitrary decision, unsupported by any biological evidence, they said, "Well, that's your point of view. This is a matter of individual conscience, and in a pluralistic society, people must be free to follow their consciences."

Unfortunately, many liberals and radicals accepted this view without further question. Perhaps many did not know that an eight-week-old fetus has a fully human form. They did not ask whether American slave-holders before the Civil War were right in viewing blacks as less than human and as private property; or whether the Nazis were correct in viewing mental patients, Jews, and Gypsies as less than human and therefore subject to the final solution.

Class issues provided another rationale. In the late 1960s, liberals were troubled by evidence that rich women could obtain abortions regardless of the law, by going to careful society doctors or to countries where abortion was legal. Why, they asked, should poor women be barred from something the wealthy could have? One might turn this argument on its head by asking why rich children should be denied protection that poor children have.

But pro-life activists did not want abortion to be a class issue one way or the other; they wanted to end abortion everywhere, for all classes. And many people who had experienced poverty did not think providing legal abortion was any favor to poor women. Thus, in 1972, when a Presidential commission on population growth recommended legalized abortion, partly to remove discrimination against poor women, several commission members dissented.

One was Graciela Olivarez, a Chicana who was active in civil rights and anti-poverty work. Olivarez, who later was named to head the Federal Government's Community Services Administration, had known poverty in her youth in the Southwest. With a touch of bitterness, she said in her dissent, "The poor cry out for justice and equality and we respond with legalized abortion." Olivarez noted that blacks and Chicanos had often been unwanted by white society. She added, "I believe that in a society that permits the life of even one individual (born or unborn) to be dependent on whether that life is 'wanted' or not, all its citizens stand in danger." Later she told the press, "We do not have equal opportunities. Abortion is a cruel way out."

Many liberals were also persuaded by a church/state argument that followed roughly this line: "Opposition to abortion is a religious viewpoint, particularly a Catholic viewpoint. The Catholics have no business imposing their religious views on the rest of us." It is true that opposition to abortion is a religious position for many people. Orthodox Jews, Mormons, and many of the fundamentalist Protestant groups also oppose abortion. (So did the mainstream Protestant churches until recent years.) But many people are against abortion for reasons that are independent of religious authority or belief. Many would still be against abortion if they lost their faith; others are opposed to it after they *have* lost their faith, or if they never had any faith. Only if their non-religious grounds for opposition can be proven baseless could legal prohibition of abortion fairly be called an establishment of religion. The pro-abortion forces concentrate heavily on religious arguments against abortion and generally ignore the secular arguments—possibly because they cannot answer them.

Still another, more emotional reason is that so many conservatives oppose abortion. Many liberals have difficulty accepting the idea that Jesse Helms can be right about *anything*. I do not quite understand this attitude. Just by the law of averages, he has to be right about something, sometime. Standing at the March for Life rally at the U.S. Capitol last year, and hearing Senator Helms say that "We reject the philosophy that life should be only for the planned, the perfect, or the privileged," I thought he was making a good civil-rights statement.

If much of the leadership of the pro-life movement is right-wing, that is due largely to the default of the Left. We "little people" who marched against the war and now march against abortion would like to see leaders of the Left speaking out on behalf of the unborn. But we see only a few, such as Dick Gregory, Mark Hatfield, Jesse Jackson, Richard Neuhaus, Mary Rose Oakar. Most of the others either avoid the issue or support abortion. We are dismayed by their inconsistency. And we are not impressed by arguments that we should work and vote for them because they are good on such issues as food stamps and medical care.

Although many liberals and radicals accepted legalized abortion, there are signs of uneasiness about it. Tell someone who supports it that you have many problems with the issue, and she is likely to say, quickly, "Oh, I don't think I could ever have one myself, but . . ." or "I'm really not pro-*abortion,* I'm *pro-choice*" or "I'm *personally* opposed to it, but. . . ."

Why are they personally opposed to it if there is nothing wrong with it?

Perhaps such uneasiness is a sign that many on the Left are ready to take another look at the abortion issue. In the hope of contributing toward a new perspective, I offer the following points:

First, it is out of character for the Left to neglect the weak and helpless. The traditional mark of the Left has been its protection of the underdog, the weak, and the poor. The unborn child is the most helpless form of humanity, even more in need of protection than the poor tenant farmer or the mental patient or the boat people on the high seas. The basic instinct of the Left is to aid those who cannot aid themselves—and that instinct is absolutely sound. It is what keeps the human proposition going.

Second, the right to life underlies and sustains every other right we have. It is, as Thomas Jefferson and his friends said, self-evident. Logically, as well as in our Declaration of Independence, it comes before the right to liberty and the right to property. The right to exist, to be free from assault by others, is the basis of equality. Without it, the other rights are meaningless, and life becomes a sort of warfare in which force decides everything. There is no equality, because one person's convenience takes precedence over another's life, provided only that the first person has more power. If we do not protect this right for everyone, it is not guaranteed for everyone, because anyone can become weak and vulnerable to assault.

Third, abortion is a civil-rights issue. Dick Gregory and many other blacks view abortion as a type of genocide. Confirmation of this comes in the experience of pro-life activists who find open bigotry when they speak with white voters about public funding of abortion. Many white voters believe abortion is a solution for the welfare problem and a way to slow the growth of the black population. I worked two years ago for a liberal, pro-life candidate who was appalled by the number of anti-black comments he found when discussing the issue. And Representative Robert Dornan of California, a conservative pro-life leader, once told his colleagues in the House, "I have heard many rock-ribbed Republicans brag about how fiscally conservative they are and then tell me that I was an idiot on the abortion issue." When he asked why, said Dornan, they whispered, "Because we have to hold them down, we have to stop the population growth." Dornan elaborated: "To them, population growth means blacks, Puerto Ricans, or other Latins," or anyone who "should not be having more than a polite one or two 'burdens on society.'"

Fourth, abortion exploits women. Many women are pressured by spouses, lovers, or parents into having abortions they do not want. Sometimes the coercion is subtle, as when a husband complains of financial problems. Sometimes it is open and crude, as when a boyfriend threatens to end the affair unless the woman has an abortion, or when parents order a minor child to have an abortion. Pro-life activists who do "clinic counseling" (standing outside abortion clinics, trying to speak to each woman who enters, urging her to have the child) report that many women who enter clinics alone are willing to talk and to listen. Some change their minds and decide against abortion. But a woman who is accompanied by someone else often does not have the chance to talk, because the husband or boyfriend or parent is so hostile to the pro-life worker.

Juli Loesch, a feminist/pacifist writer, notes that feminists want to have men participate more in the care of children, but abortion allows a man to shift total responsibility to the woman: "He can *buy* his way out of accountability by making 'The Offer' for 'The Procedure.'" She adds that the man's sexual role "then implies—exactly nothing: no relationship. How quickly a 'woman's right to choose' comes to serve a 'man's right to use.'" And Daphne de Jong, a New Zealand feminist, says, "If women must submit to abortion to preserve their lifestyle or career, their economic or social status, they are pandering to a system devised and run by men for male convenience." She adds, "Of all the things which are done to women to fit them into a society dominated by men, abortion is the most violent invasion of their physical and psychic integrity. It is a deeper and more destructive assault than rape. . . ."

Loesch, de Jong, Olivarez, and other pro-life feminists believe men should bear a much greater share of the burdens of child-rearing than they do at present. And de Jong makes a radical point when she says, "Accepting short-term solutions like abortion only delays the implementation of real reforms like decent maternity and paternity leaves, job protection, high-quality child care, community responsibility for dependent people of all ages, and recognition of the economic contribution of child-minders." Olivarez and others have also called for the development of safer and more effective contraceptives for both men and women. In her 1972 dissent, Olivarez noted with irony that "medical science has developed four different ways for killing a fetus, but has not yet developed a safe-for-all-to-use contraceptive."

Fifth, abortion is an escape from an obligation that is owed to another. Doris Gordon, Coordinator of Libertarians for Life, puts it this way: "Unborn children don't cause women to become pregnant but parents cause their children to be in the womb, and as a result, they need parental care. As a general principle, if we are the cause of another's need for care, as when we cause an accident, we acquire an obligation to that person as a result. . . . We have no right to kill in order to terminate any obligation."

Sixth, abortion brutalizes those who perform it, undergo it, pay for it, profit from it, and allow it to happen. Those who look the other way because they do not want to think about abortion are like those who refused to think about Vietnam. A part of reality is blocked out because one does not want to see broken bodies coming home, or going to an incinerator, in those awful plastic bags. People deny their own humanity when they refuse to identify with, or even acknowledge, the pain of others.

With some it is worse: They are making money from the misery of others, from exploited women and dead children. Doctors, businessmen, and clinic directors are making a great deal of money from abortion. Jobs and high incomes depend on abortion; it's part of the gross national product. The parallels of this with the military-industrial complex should be obvious to anyone who was involved in the anti-war movement.

And the "slippery slope" argument is right: People really do go from accepting abortion to accepting euthanasia and accepting "triage" for the world hunger problem and accepting "life-boat ethics" as a general guide to human behavior. We slip down the slope, back to the jungle.

To save the smallest children, and to save its own conscience, the Left should speak out against abortion.

The Indivisibility of Life and the Slippery Slope

Nat Hentoff

This was a speech given to the Americans United for Life Forum in Chicago on October 18, 1986, published in Harmony *magazine, vol. 1, no. 4. Nat Hentoff is a columnist for the* Village Voice *and also writes for the* Progressive *and similar publications. He has published several books, and focuses on freedom of speech issues.*

I'll begin by indicating how I became aware, very belatedly, of the "indivisibility of life." I mention this fragment of autobiography only because I think it may be useful to those who are interested in bringing others like me . . . to a realization that the "slippery slope" is far more than a metaphor.

When I say "like me" I suppose in some respects I'm regarded as a "liberal," although I often stray from that category, and certainly a civil libertarian—though the ACLU and I are in profound disagreement on the matters of abortion, handicapped infants and euthanasia, because I think they have forsaken the basic civil liberties in dealing with those issues. I'm considered a liberal except for that unaccountable heresy of recent years that has to do with pro-life matters.

It's all the more unaccountable to a lot of people because I remain an atheist, a Jewish atheist. (That's a special branch of the division.) I think the question I'm most often asked from both sides is, "How do you presume to have this kind of moral conception without a belief in God?" And the answer is "It's harder." But it's not impossible. For me, this transformation started with the reporting I did on the Babies Doe. While covering the story, I came across a number of physicians, medical writers, staff people in Congress and some members of the House and Senate who were convinced that making it possible for a spina bifida or a Down's syndrome infant to die was the equivalent of what they called "late abortion." And surely, they felt, there's nothing wrong with that.

Now, I had not been thinking about abortion at all. I had what W. H. Auden called in another context a "rehearsed response." You mentioned abortion and I would say "Oh yeah, that's a fundamental part of women's liberation," and that was the end of it.

But then I started hearing about "late abortion." The simple "fact" that the infant had been born, proponents suggest, should not get in the way of mercifully saving him or her from a life hardly worth living. At the same time, the parents are saved from the financial and emotional burden of caring for an imperfect child.

And then I heard the head of the Reproductive Freedom Rights unit of the ACLU saying at a forum (this was at the same time as the Baby Jane Doe story was developing on Long Island), "I don't know what all this fuss is about. Dealing with these handicapped infants is really an extension of women's reproductive rights, women's rights to control their own bodies."

That stopped me. It seemed to me that we were not talking about *Roe v. Wade*. These infants were *born*. And having been born, as persons under the Constitution, they were entitled to at least the same rights as people on death row—due process, equal protection of the law. So for the first time, I began to pay attention to the "slippery slope" warnings of pro-lifers I read about or had seen on television. Because abortion had become legal and easily available, that argument ran—as you well know—infanticide would eventually become openly permissible, to be followed by euthanasia for infirm, expensive senior citizens.

And then in the *New York Review of Books*, I saw the respected, though not by me, Australian bio-ethicist Peter Singer assert that the slope was not slippery at all, but rather a logical throughway once you got to it. This is what he said—and I've heard this in variant forms from many, many people who consider themselves compassionate, concerned with the powerless and all that.

Singer: "The pro-life groups were right about one thing, the location of the baby inside or outside the womb cannot make much of a moral difference. We cannot coherently hold it is all right to kill a fetus a week before birth, but as soon as the baby is born everything must be done to keep it alive. The solution is the very opposite, to abandon the idea that all human life is of equal worth." Which, of course, the majority of the Court had already done in *Roe* v. *Wade*.

Recently, I was interviewing Dr. Norman Levinsky, Chief of Medicine of Boston University Medical Center and a medical ethicist. He is one of those rare medical ethicists who really is concerned with nurturing life, as contrasted with those of his peers who see death as a form of treatment.

He told me that he is much disturbed by the extent to which medical decisions are made according to the patient's age. He says there are those physicians who believe that life is worth less if you're over 80 than if you're 28.

So this is capsulizing an incremental learning process. I was beginning to learn about the indivisibility of life. I began to interview people, to read, and I read Dr. Leo Alexander. Joe Stanton, who must be the greatest single resource of information, at least to beginners—and, I think, non-beginners—in this field, sent me a whole lot of stuff, including Dr. Alexander's piece in the *New England Journal of Medicine* in the 1940's. And then I thought of Dr. Alexander when I saw an April 1984 piece in the *New England Journal of Medicine* by 10 physicians defending the withdrawal of food and water from certain "hopelessly ill" patients. And I found out that Dr. Alexander was still alive then but didn't have much longer to live. And he said to Patrick Durr, who is a professor of philosophy at Clarke University and who testified in the Brophy case, about that article, "It is much like Germany in the 20s and 30s. The barriers against killing are coming down."

Nearly two years later, as you know, the seven member judicial council of the American Medical Association ruled unanimously that it is ethical for doctors to withhold "all means of life-prolonging medical treatment" including food and water, if the patient is in a coma that is "beyond doubt irreversible" and there are "adequate safeguards to confirm the accuracy of the diagnosis." Death, to begin with, may not be imminent for food and water to be stopped, according to the AMA.

Then Dr. Nancy Dickey, who is chairman of the council that made that ruling, noted that there is no medical definition of "adequate safeguards," no checklist that doctors would have to fill out in each case. The decision would be up to each doctor.

Aside from the ethics of this, for the moment, I would like to point out that the *New England Journal of Medicine,* or at least the editor, Dr. Arnold Relman, said fairly recently that there are at least 40,000 incompetent physicians in the United States—incompetent or impaired. At least.

Back to Dr. Norman Levinsky. This is all part of the learning process. It is not a huge step, he said, from stopping the feeding to giving the patient a little more morphine to speed his end. I mean it is not a big step from passive to active euthanasia.

Well, in time, a rather short period of time, I became pro-life across the board, which led to certain problems, starting at home. My wife's most recurrent attack begins with "You are creating social mischief," and there are people who do not speak to me anymore. In most cases, that's no loss.

And I began to find out, in a different way, how the stereotypes about pro-lifers work. When you're one of them and you read about the stereotypes, you get a sort of different perspective.

There's a magazine called the *Progressive*. It's published in Madison, Wisconsin. It comes out of the progressive movement of Senator Lafayette, in the early part of this century. It is very liberal. Its staff, the last I knew, was without exception pro-abortion. But its editor is a rare editor in that he believes not only that his readers can stand opinions contrary to what they'd like to hear, but that it's good for them. His name is Erwin Knoll and he published a long piece by Mary Meehan,[1] who is one of my favorite authors, which pointed out that for the left, of all groups of society, not to understand that the most helpless members of this society are the preborn—a word that I picked up today, better than unborn—is strange, to say the least.

The article by Meehan produced an avalanche of letters. I have not seen such vitriol since Richard Nixon was president—and he deserved it. One of the infuriated said pro-life is only a code word representing the kind of neo-fascist, absolutist thinking that is the antithesis to the goals of the left. What, exactly, are the anti-abortionists for? School prayer, a strong national defense, the traditional family characterized by patriarchal dominance. And what are they against? School busing, homosexuals, divorce, sex education, the ERA, welfare, contraception and birth control. I read that over five or six times and none of those applied to me.

I began to wonder if Meehan and I were the only pro-life people who came from the left. Meehan has a long background in civil rights work. And by the way, she said in the piece, "It is out of character for the left to neglect the weak and helpless. The traditional mark of the left has been its protection of the underdog, the weak and the poor. The unborn child is the most helpless form of humanity, even more in need of protection than the poor tenant farmer or the medical patient. The basic instinct of the left is to aid those who cannot aid themselves. And that instinct is absolutely sound. It's what keeps the human proposition going."

I'll give you a quick footnote on the *Progressive*. Erwin Knoll got a series of ads, tiny ads because they couldn't pay very much even at the magazine's rates, from a group called Feminists for Life of America—a group, by the way, that is anti-nuclear weapons and is also very pro-life in terms of being anti-abortion. And the ads ran. There is a group called the Funding Exchange which is made up of foundations which are put into operation and headed by scions of the rich. These are children who are trying to atone for their parents' rapaciousness by doing good. The children are liberals. The Funding Exchange was so horrified to see those three tiny ads that even though the *Progressive* is soundly pro-abortion, the Funding Exchange not only dropped the grant they had given the *Progressive,* but they made a point of telling Erwin Knoll that they were going to make sure that other foundations didn't give them any money either. I'm always intrigued at how few people understand that free speech encompasses a little more than speech you like.

Well, eventually, in addition to Mary Meehan, I found that there were a number of other pro-lifers who also do not cherish the MX missile, William Bradford Reynolds, or Ronald Reagan. And one of them is Juli Loesch, who writes and speaks against both war and abortion. She is the founder of Pro-lifers for Survival, which describes itself as a network of women and men supporting alternatives to abortion and nuclear arms.

She's rather rare, I find in my limited experience, among combatants on all sides of this question, because she is unfailingly lucid—and she has a good sense of humor. In an interview in the U.S. Catholic she said that combining her various pro-life preoccupations "was the most fun I've ever had in my life. It's great because you always have common ground with someone. For example, if you're talking to pro-lifers you can always warm up the crowd, so to speak, by saying a lot of anti-abortion stuff. After you've got everybody celebrating the principles they all hold dear, you apply those principles to the nuclear arms issue. For instance, I'll say 'this nuclear radiation is going to destroy the unborn in the womb all over the world.' And then I always lay a quote by the late Herman Kahn on them. He pointed out that about 100 million embryonic deaths would result from limited nuclear war. One hundred million embryonic deaths is of limited significance, he said, because human fecundity being what it is, the slight reduction in fecundity should not be a matter of serious concern even to individuals. Tell that to a pro-life group," she says, "and their response will be, 'That guy's an abortionist.' Well what he was was a nuclear strategist."

I found other allies as a result of having been interviewed on National Public Radio as the curiosity of the month. Letters came in from around the country, most of them saying essentially what a woman from Illinois wrote: "I feel as you do, that it is ethically, not to mention logically, inconsistent to oppose capital punishment and nuclear armament while supporting abortion and/or euthanasia."

The most surprising letters were two from members of the boards of two state affiliates of the ACLU. Now I'm a former member of the national board and I was on the New York board for 17 years, and I well know the devotion of the vast number of the rank and file, let alone the leadership, to abortion rights. So I was surprised to get these letters. One board member from Maryland said we had a board meeting where we approved with only one dissent (his) the decision of the national board to put the right to abortion at the top of its priorities—the top of its priorities. Forget the First Amendment and the Fourth, let Edwin Meese take care of those. There was no discussion, he said, of the relation of abortion to capital punishment.

The most interesting letter was from Barry Nakell, who is a law professor at the University of North Carolina. He is one of the founders of the affiliate of the ACLU there, and he gave me a copy of a speech he made in 1985 at the annual meeting in Chapel Hill of the North Carolina Civil Liberties Union. He reminded the members that the principle of respect for the dignity of life was the basis for the paramount issue on the North Carolina Civil Liberties Union agenda since its founding. That group was founded because of their opposition to capital punishment. Yet, he said, supporting *Roe* v. *Wade,* these civil libertarians were agreeing that the Constitution protects the right to take life. The situation is a little backward, Nakell told his brothers and sisters. In the classical position, the Constitution would be interpreted to protect the right to life, and pro-abortion advocates would be pressing to relax that constitutional guarantee. In *Roe* v. *Wade,* the Supreme Court turned that position upside down and the ACLU went along, taking the decidedly odd civil libertarian position that some lives are less worthy of protection than other lives. I asked Nakell how his heresy had been received. Apparently they're much more polite down there than they are in New York. "With civility," he said. As a matter of fact, he added, there were several members of the board who had been troubled for some time, but it's interesting, they didn't quite want to come out and say they were worried about *Roe* v. *Wade,* that they were worried about abortion . . .

For several years now I've been researching a profile of Cardinal O'Connor of New York, which will be a book eventually. And in the course of that I came across Cardinal Bernardin's "seamless garment" concept. It's a phrase he does not use any more because of internal political reasons. It is now called the "consistent ethic of life" which is fine by me. I miss "seamless garment" though, because there's a nice literary flavor to it. But I'll accept "consistent ethic of life." Bernardin said, in a speech at Fordham that has won him considerable plaudits and considerable dissonance, "Nuclear war threatens life on a previously unimaginable scale. Abortion takes life daily on a horrendous scale. Public executions are fast becoming weekly events in the most advanced technological society in history, and euthanasia is now openly discussed and even advocated. Each of these assaults on life has its own meaning and morality. They cannot be collapsed into one problem, but they must be confronted as pieces of a larger pattern."

That had a profound effect on me. It's not new. As a matter of fact, Juli Loesch thought of it before he did, as did the people at *The Catholic Worker* who got it, of course, from Dorothy Day. And it goes further back into the centuries. But there was something about the way Bernardin put it that hit me very hard.

So I decided by now, because I was considered by some people to be a reliable pro-lifer, I decided to go out to Columbus, Ohio where I had been asked to speak at the annual Right to Life convention. And, I thought, I'm going to bring them the word, if they haven't heard it before from Cardinal Bernardin. At first they were delighted to see me, but that didn't last very long. Jack Willke and Mrs. Willke were there, and they can attest to the fact that in some respects I'm lucky to be here. I pointed out that pro-lifers—maybe this is chutzpah, telling people who have been in this all their lives what you've discovered in 20 minutes—that pro-lifers ought to be opposing capital punishment and nuclear armament and the Reagan budget with its dedicated care for missiles, as it cuts funds for Women/Infant/Children program that provides diet supplements and medical checkups for mothers in poverty. Surely, I said, they should not emulate the President in these matters—and here I stole a line from Congressman Barney Frank—they should not emulate the President in being pro-life only up to the moment of birth. Well the faces before me began to close, and from the middle and the back of the dining room there were shouts. I couldn't make out the words, but they were not approving. As I went on, there were more shouts as well as growls and table-thumping of an insistence that indicated a tumbrel awaited outside. I finally ended my speech to a chorus of howls, and several of the diners rushed toward the dais. I did not remember ever intending to die for this cause, but as it turned out the attacks were all verbal. Most of the disappointed listeners, once they caught their breath, charitably ascribed my failure to understand the total unrelatedness of nuclear arms and abortion to my not yet having found God.

But I discovered in other places that I didn't have to bring them the news of the consistent ethic of life. I talked at the Catholic church outside Stamford,

Connecticut last week, and they—including the pastor—understood the "consistent ethic of life" a great deal better than I did. So I see some real hope for my point of view. . . .

Most people will begin to understand the lethal logic of the abortionists, the doctors of euthanasia, and the AMA, if this logic is presented lucidly, persistently, and on the basis of the indivisibility of all life. All life.

NOTE AND REFERENCE

1. This article is republished as Chapter 2 in this book.

Israel/Palestine and Abortion

Stephen Zunes

Perhaps no two issues create greater polarization in American politics today than abortion and the Israeli-Palestinian conflict. As a scholar and activist long opposed to the Israeli occupation of Arab lands seized in the 1967 war as part of a consistent ethic supporting human rights, I identify with activists opposing abortion as part of a consistent ethic supporting life.

On both issues, the debate has become simplistic and polarized. Special interests make it difficult for political leaders to take courageous stands based on moral principles.

On both issues we find ourselves yelled at and falsely labeled by otherwise rational, liberal-minded people.

Even opposing Israeli policies out of a general moral opposition to any country invading, occupying, colonizing, and oppressing another will often be assumed to instead be based upon Israel being the world's only Jewish state. Since the right-wing Israeli government has convinced many that controlling the West Bank is necessary for the country's survival, opposing the occupation is depicted as not caring whether Israel is destroyed, and therefore indicates anti-Semitic attitudes.

Similarly, even if one opposes abortion out of a general moral opposition to violence against any human being, some assume opposition is instead based upon the belief that women should be used as chattel and denied basic rights. Since the movement for legalized abortion has convinced many that unrestricted access to abortion is necessary for women's emancipation and equality, opposing abortion comes across as a desire to relegate women to traditional sex roles and therefore indicates sexism and misogyny.

Rational people normally do not act so angrily and defensively unless there are deep-seated hurts inside making it difficult to think more clearly. In both cases, there is genuine fear. For many Jews, a militarily dominant Israel represents a necessary defense of the only sanctuary for their oppressed brothers and sisters long denied a homeland of their own, who for centuries experienced waves of persecution to the point of genocide. For women, legalized abortion represents a means of escaping unplanned motherhood, which for centuries forced women into the role of primary parent and homemaker with minimal economic or emotional support, thereby denying them the right to pursue their own dreams.

For supporters of both the Israeli occupation and legalized abortion, any sense that the means of escape from centuries of oppression is under attack can bring to the surface primal fears. Honest political differences on the best means of protecting the rights of Jews or women can come across, at least on an emotional level, as nothing less than a challenge to one's survival.

Such fears are not rational. Yet, if one examines many of those in the movement against abortion and opposing the Israeli occupation, it becomes apparent that such fears do not come out of nowhere.

Many critics of the Israeli occupation really are using the Palestinian cause as an excuse to promote an anti-Semitic agenda. Similarly, many of those in the antiabortion movement really are using the issue as an excuse to promote a misogynist agenda.

It is doubtful most right-wing American politicians who oppose abortion really care about the welfare of the unborn, given their poor record regarding the welfare of children already born. Similarly, it is doubtful most Arab leaders who oppose the Israeli occupation care much about the human rights of Palestinians, given their poor record regarding the human rights of their own citizens. Such opportunism and hypocrisy facilitate supporters of the Israeli occupation or legalized abortion in dismissing the underlying legitimate concerns.

Those who disingenuously take on these respective causes do so because it serves their purposes of addressing an issue which many correctly recognize as a moral travesty. This deflects popular resentment against their support for unjust policies, ultimately driven by powerful and wealthy interests, and serves to refocus it onto historically disempowered groups—women and Jews.

The dilemma is that in defending the rights of Palestinians or unborn children, we challenge policies supposedly taken for the benefit of other historically oppressed groups. In doing so, we sometimes find ourselves in the company of those who are using these policies as an excuse to perpetuate the very oppression these policies are supposedly trying to overcome. Unless you know an individual activist personally, it is sometimes difficult to discern what is actually motivating him or her.

When I overhear a conversation with someone talking negatively about the oppressive policies of the Israeli government, I am initially concerned—even if I agree with everything being said—about what actually motivates their opposition. Does this person also oppose Morocco's occupation of Western Sahara and other foreign military occupations? Is this person's concern about Palestinians part of a universal commitment to human rights, international law, self-determination, and justice? Or, is this person using Israel's reprehensible policies as an excuse to bash the world's only Jewish state?

Many Jews and others sensitive to anti-Semitism accordingly are reluctant to publicly criticize Israeli policies for fear it would encourage such bigotry. The effect, however, could be the opposite. If those of us who do care about Israel's security do not criticize Israeli actions for the right reasons, it will be left to anti-Semites who criticize Israel for the wrong reasons.

Similarly, when I overhear a conversation with someone talking negatively about the violence of abortion, I am concerned initially—again, even if I am in full agreement—about what motivates this opposition. Does this person also oppose other forms of legalized violence such as capital punishment and war? Is this person concerned about ending all forms of violence in society? Or is this person using the tragedy of abortion as an excuse to challenge those who seek to overcome sexism, homophobia, and other oppressive cultural norms and to assert rights of individuals in their moral choices?

Many people with serious moral qualms about abortion but not wanting to unwittingly promote a reactionary social agenda therefore remain silent. This is also a poor strategy. The timidity of many progressives with antiabortion sentiments to speak out has led to much of the movement becoming dominated by right-wing opportunists who oppose abortion for the wrong reasons.

Just as those of us who work to support Palestinian rights must recognize the legitimate concerns of Israelis and acknowledge the sin of anti-Semitism which has led Israel to commit such horrific violence against Palestinians, we who oppose abortion must also recognize the legitimate concerns of women and the sin of sexism which lead so many women to make the terrible choice to end the lives of their unborn children.

What I have learned through my support for Palestinian rights and opposition to the Israeli occupation is the importance of distancing myself from those who do not approach the issue from the point of view of a consistent ethic of human rights and international law. I therefore reiterate my support for Israel's right to exist in peace and security, my opposition to terrorism in all forms, and my acknowledgement of the manifold failures of Palestinian and other Arab leaders. I avoid participating in demonstrations or forums with those who do not share these universal principles, except where I believe I might be able to push people into adopting a more consistent ethic. I emphasize that—if the goal is to support Israeli security and safety for Jews—Israeli policy is having the opposite effect.

Right-wing Jewish leaders in Israel and the United States have played on the fears of their constituencies in giving the false impression that increasing Israel's militarism and repression enhances the security of Jews in Israel and elsewhere when, in reality, the occupation fuels terrorism. Hamas, Islamic Jihad, and the Al-Aqsa Martyrs Brigade did not even exist until after years of Israeli occupation and the failure of Israelis to end their colonization drive and occupation of Palestinian lands taken in June 1967. The Palestine Authority and all neighboring Arab states have agreed to security guarantees and full diplomatic relations in return for a total Israeli withdrawal. Israeli progressives, and a growing number of nonideological pragmatists, stress that Israeli security and Palestinian rights are not mutually exclusive, but mutually dependent on the other. Israel will be far more secure with a functional demilitarized Palestinian state on its borders than trying to suppress or encircle nearly two million people in noncontiguous cantons without freedom of movement or the ability to build an economically viable nation-state.

I also argue that only when Israel sees its future with the Third World—made necessary by its geography, its Semitic language and culture, its sizable Sephardic population, and the Jews' history of exploitation by the Europeans—will Israel end its isolation and find the real security it seeks. Many of the so-called supporters of Israel in American politics actually make Israel vulnerable by tying its future to an imperial agenda and blocking its more natural alliance with the world's Afro-Asian majority. The combination of Israeli technology, Palestinian industriousness and entrepreneurship, and Arabian oil wealth could result in an economic, political, and social transformation of the Middle East which would benefit the region's inhabitants, but not those who profit from continued divisions between Semitic peoples. Meanwhile, Israeli leaders and their counterparts in many American Zionist organizations are repeating the historic error of trading short-term benefits at the risk of long-term security.

Israel would not have been able to maintain its occupation of the West Bank were it not for the massive arms transfers, economic subsidies, and diplomatic support by the United States. The United States, far from being an honest broker, has consistently sided with Israel on outstanding issues in the peace process and has blocked the international community from effectively challenging Israel's ongoing violations of the United Nations Charter, the Fourth Geneva Convention and a series of UN Security Council resolutions. An Israel in a constant state of war is far more willing to serve as a market for American weapons and cooperate as a strategic partner in this important region than an Israel at peace with its neighbors.

One of the more unsettling aspects of the U.S. policy is how closely it corresponds with historic anti-Semitism. Throughout Europe in past centuries, the ruling class would, in return for granting limited religious and cultural autonomy, set up certain Jews as its visible agents, such as tax collectors and moneylenders. When the population threatened to revolt against the rulers, the rulers could then blame the Jews, sending the wrath of an exploited people against convenient scapegoats, resulting in pogroms and other notorious waves of repression throughout the Jewish Diaspora. The idea behind Zionism was to break this cycle through the creation of a Jewish nation-state, where Jews would no longer be dependent on the ruling class and other countries. The tragic irony is that, because of Israel's unwillingness to make peace with its Arab neighbors, this cycle is being perpetrated on a global scale. Israel is being used by Western imperialist powers to maintain their interests in the Middle East. Therefore, autocratic Arab governments and other Third World regimes blame "Zionism" for their problems rather than the broader exploitative global economic system and their own elites.

This cycle can only be broken when current American policy is challenged and Israelis and Palestinians are finally allowed to settle their differences and join together in liberating the Middle East from both Western imperialism and their own short-sighted rulers.

Rather than enhancing Israel's legitimate security interests, the occupation actually harms Israeli security. Similarly, rather than enhancing the liberation of women, legitimizing abortion actually harms women's rights.

Just as Europeans pushed the "Jewish problem" onto the Palestinians instead of dealing with their anti-Semitism, our patriarchal political leaders make abortion available instead of dealing with male responsibility for unplanned pregnancies. Legitimizing abortion relieves the pressure on government and society to improve day care facilities with adequate staffing and funding; provide extended paid parental leaves; offer flexible working hours and schooling options for single parents; offer improved sex education in the schools and elsewhere; make available more effective, safer, and available contraception;

provide universal health care; streamline adoption procedures; restore aid to families with dependent children through procedures which uphold the dignity of the recipients; end graphic rape in advertising, the spread of pornography and other means by which the media promotes disrespectful sexuality without parallel education on its consequences; and provide more public education and training against date rape and other forms of coercive or semicoercive sexual activities where women are denied a true choice, and therefore often lack adequate safeguards against pregnancy.

There need not be a contradiction between family and career. There are scores of countries around the world, most of which are less wealthy than the United States, where lengthy paid maternal (and often paternal) leaves are available, child care is available at work sites, and breaks are allowed during the day for nursing.

Legalized abortion gives the illusion of women having control over their own bodies while it is still unsafe for women to walk on the streets at night in most urban areas, images of graphic rape still plague the media, men still use women sexually as outlets for their aggression and domination, and social norms still force many women to meet men's desires in dress and appearance.

Neither women nor Jews are the greatest perpetrators of violence and injustice in the world, and yet they have become the principal targets of many who claim to be concerned with violence and injustice. It may not be a conscious bigotry that motivates such misplaced priorities. Perhaps it is a bit too scary to recognize that tackling the underlying violence and injustice means taking on far more powerful institutions. To successfully challenge the Israeli occupation means taking on U.S. imperialism. To successfully stop abortion means taking on patriarchy and powerful economic interests. There is an old joke on why animal rights activists tend to go after those who wear fur more than those who wear leather: it is safer to harass old ladies than bikers.

We must be willing to look at the big picture, however. Those of us in the consistent pro-life movement should be open and inclusive to a wide range of perspectives and ideologies. At the same time, while recognizing that abortion is indeed an act of violence, we must also be aware that it is fundamentally a symptom of an unjust system, and that addressing the root causes of the violence around us may require fundamental and radical changes to the economic, social, and political system that makes it possible.

Understanding How Killing Traumatizes the Killer

Rachel M. MacNair

"I have fetus dreams, we all do here: dreams of abortions one after the other; of buckets of blood splashed on the walls; trees full of crawling fetuses. I dreamed that two men grabbed me and began to drag me away. 'Let's do an abortion,' they said with a sickening leer, and I began to scream, plunged into a vision of sucking, scraping pain . . ."[1]

—*Sallie Tisdale, an abortion nurse who was still pro-choice*

"Now at night when I lie down, I start up with a roar as victim after victim comes up before me. I can see them on the trap, waiting a second before they face their Maker. They haunt me and taunt me until I am nearly crazy with an unearthly fear."[2]

—*Former Canadian executioner John Robert Radclive*

"Can you give me an explanation for this, doctor: as soon as someone goes against me I want to hit him. Even outside my job. I feel I want to settle the fellows who get in my way, even for nothing at all . . . suppose I go to the kiosk to buy the papers . . . I hold out my hand (the chap who keeps the kiosk is a pal of mine) to take my papers. Someone in the line gives me a challenging look and says 'Wait your turn.' Well, I feel I want to beat him up and I say to myself, 'If I had you for a few hours my fine fellow you wouldn't look so clever afterwards.'"[3]

—*Psychiatric case of a French police officer in Algeria whose job included torture*

"I don't sleep for the week after."[4]

—*An anonymous Dutch doctor, speaking of euthanasia cases*

Post-traumatic Stress Disorder (PTSD) is the professional term for a pattern of symptoms that used to be called combat fatigue, battle fatigue, or shell shock. During the U.S. Civil War, it was regarded as cowardice and treated contemptuously. During World War I, it was commonly thought to come from shell sounds and to be physical in origin. German psychiatrists thought it was caused by a desire for compensation and treated it cruelly, putting men back into combat. By World War II, its origin was finally recognized as psychological, resulting from suffering a trauma, and treated accordingly. With the American war in Vietnam, the numbers grew, along with the lobby for treating veterans more seriously. By 1980, it had an official name and now has two official definitions, one from the American Psychiatric Association and one from the World Health Organization. Thousands of research articles have been written on it.

Yet, people still mainly think of PTSD as caused entirely by being a victim: The soldier was scared of being shot, the soldier was grieved over buddies being shot. The idea that the act of shooting could be traumatizing to the soldier rarely occurred to researchers.

In the mid-1990s, I contemplated that if abortion is killing, as opponents claim, rather than a mere medical procedure, as many of its defenders claim, then would it not follow that those who perform it would have the same reaction as those who do what everyone agrees is killing? I knew that the current name for battle fatigue was PTSD, but in my peace activist innocence, I assumed people understood this as a reaction to killing—that is what battles are after all. For years I searched, fearing I simply had not located the articles or books that would be the mother lode of scholarship on this idea. There actually was one area where there were many such articles—police officers who shoot in the line of duty. That exception is explained by the sentiment that it was the criminal, not the officer, who is seen as being to blame, so that the officer's negative reaction is still part of his or her heroic standing. The soldier or executioner is more likely to be expected to take killing in stride as part of the job.

Whatever little I did find suggested that PTSD symptoms would be more severe for killing. This was a pioneering area of research, and I needed to pull together scattered scholarship on all the groups expected to commit socially approved acts of violence and launch the concept in a book. The book came out in 2002, entitled *Perpetration-Induced Traumatic Stress: The Psychological Consequences of Killing* (Praeger). This form of PTSD symptoms caused by killing or other acts of violence has the acronym PITS.

COLD-HEARTED NUMBERS

As part of that book, I researched the U.S. government data on its Vietnam veterans, a large, stratified collection of random samples collected in the 1980s. Those who say they killed had more severe PTSD than those who say they did not, and those who were "directly involved" in situations of killing civilians had higher PTSD scores than those who "only saw" such situations. In fact, those who said they killed under any circumstances had higher scores than those who "only saw."

Nor was it only that they were in more intense battle. Those who killed in light combat had heavier PTSD scores than those who did not kill even though they were in heavy combat.

The pattern showed that those who say they killed report experiencing much more intrusive imagery—nightmares, flashbacks, and unwanted thoughts that would not go away. They also reported more irritable outbursts, as illustrated by the case of the French police officer mentioned earlier. They tended to have higher scores on alienation, hypervigilance, and feelings of disintegration.

A higher percentage of soldiers in the American war in Vietnam killed than those in previous wars. Several studies show that throughout history, only 15–25 percent of soldiers have overcome the natural inclination against killing. Vietnam differed because the U.S. military was aware of this problem and solved it by better training. Bull's-eye targets do not fly around battlefields, so they used more realistic human-shaped targets that dropped when hit. With this conditioning, the firing rate went way up. If killing is not only traumatic, but more traumatic than being a victim, then it would follow that the PTSD rate among American veterans of that war would be much higher than before.

As of now, there are no number-based studies found showing psychological aftereffects in executioners or participants in euthanasia; we rely on individual stories for them. For abortion, however, there are two studies published by researchers who do not themselves work in the field of abortion, who favor abortion, and whose sample size being studied is fairly large.

One, from 1974, noted that in people involved in performing abortions, "obsessional thinking about abortion, depression, fatigue, anger, lowered self-esteem, and identity conflicts were prominent. The symptom complex was considered a 'transient reactive disorder,' similar to 'combat fatigue.'" The numbers: "sixty-six questionnaires were distributed, and forty-two were returned . . . In this particular sample, almost all professionals involved in abortion work reacted with more or less negative feelings."[5] Those having contact with the fetal remains have more negative feelings, as would be expected if abortion practice is traumatizing: "[A]mong the group of professionals who had fetus contact, there was very little variability in emotional response: All emotional reactions were unanimously extremely negative." This figure comes not from right-to-life propaganda but from an article concerned with easing the problem, in order to make abortion workers more available. This one sample, with two-thirds responding, taken by sympathizers of abortion, found negative emotions among all workers with fetal contact.

The second study is larger, with interviews of 130 abortion workers in San Francisco in 1984 and 1985.[6] It did not mention PTSD but listed symptoms similar to it: "Ambivalent periods were characterized by a variety of otherwise uncharacteristic feelings and behavior including withdrawal from colleagues, resistance to going to work, lack of energy, impatience with clients and an overall sense of uneasiness. Nightmares, images that could not be shaken and preoccupation were commonly reported. Also common was the deep and lonely privacy within which practitioners had grappled with their ambivalence." The study did not report the prevalence of the symptoms, only noting they were widespread. The authors were more concerned that, even when limited to clearly pro-choice staff, the theme of destruction arose 77 percent of the time and the word "murder" was used by 18 percent of respondents.

DREAMS

Dreams from trauma often seem like videotapes, replaying the incident. Experiencing the horror as in nightmares is also common. Additionally, two other motifs among those who have killed may be peculiar to them.

Being Accused by the People One Has Killed

One therapist cites a combat veteran who "frequently hears the voices of the Vietnamese women and children he killed, accusing him (in English) of killing them or demanding of him the explanation of why he killed them. The voices warn him that bad things will happen to himself and his family."[7]

A journalist reported on a conference of the National Abortion Federation: "They talk about . . . their dreams, in which aborted fetuses stare at them with ancient eyes and perfectly shaped hands and feet asking, 'Why? Why did you do this to me?' "[8]

Becoming a Victim of the Violence One Has Perpetrated

From an American veteran of Vietnam: "I was riding on some kind of vehicle—a bus, I think—down Fifth Avenue. Somehow it turned into a military truck—and the truck got bigger and bigger, until it reached an enormous size. I was a soldier on the truck—and I fell off . . . and was killed. [In another dream] I was riding on a subway—underground—and somehow I seemed to turn into a solider in uniform . . . There was a lot of confusion and then there was a battle with the police . . . in which I was killed."[9]

From another such veteran: "I was arguing with myself. Then there were two separate selves, and one of them finally shot the other, so that I shot myself."[10]

In the Stanford Prison Experiment, which simulated a prison and spiraled down into a highly dehumanized situation, one researcher had the following dream:

> On one of the nights that it was my turn to sleep overnight at the prison, I had a terribly realistic dream in which I was suddenly imprisoned by guards in an actual prison . . . Some of the prisoners in our study, the ones who in retrospect had impressed me as most in distress, were now decked out in elaborately militaristic guard uniforms. They were my most angry and abusive captors, and I had the unmistakable sense that there was to be no escape or release from this awful place. I awoke drenched in sweat and shaken from the experience.[11]

Note the first quotation at the beginning of the chapter. An abortion nurse, still committed to abortion as necessary, starts first with the babies, but turns quickly to what abortion does to the women—close to a rape motif. She is sensing not only the deathly violence to fetuses, but in her dreams is also understanding the violence to the women and feeling it enacted on herself.

In all cases, if they are still lodged in violent situations, the dreamers continue doing the activity causing the dreams. It would hardly be surprising that they mainly do not want to talk about it. This helps explain why we hear about it so infrequently.

NUMBING

One of the symptoms of PTSD is emotional numbing and a sense of detachment or estrangement from others. This could be a defense mechanism against memories of killing. For executions, the chaplain of Potosi prison was discussing postexecution feelings with an officer who had participated in carrying them out. He reports "I said, 'How do you feel?' And he said, 'Blank.' I said, "Blank? That's it?' And he said, *'That's all I'm feeling. Blank.'* There's nothing there. You keep thinking there's going to be some emotion. You're searching for something. . . . It's just a blank."[12] Robert Johnson found a similar reaction in an officer who told him, "I just cannot feel anything. And that was what bothered me. I thought I would feel something, but I didn't feel anything."[13]

In abortion, several reports come from those who have left; this symptom's nature suggests it would be more noticed by those who are no longer there. There is this, however, from nurse Tisdale's writing in *Harper's*: "There is a numbing sameness lurking in this job; the same questions, the same answers, even the same trembling tone in the voices . . . Still, I've cultivated a certain disregard. It isn't negligence, but I don't always pay attention."

Several other symptoms are interesting but I mention this one to highlight the quality of medical treatment. With numbing, lethal injection or abortion will have less rigorous medical care. The idea these practices can be made humane or "safe" with appropriate legal safeguards does not take into account this basic reaction of the mind of those expected to commit violence.

THE THRILL OF THE KILL

> *"It's hard to duplicate this high with drugs, except the only drug I know is cocaine, that would reproduce this high for you, the same type of high of killing."*[14]
>
> —*A case study of an American combat veteran of Vietnam*

> *"Combat addiction . . . is caused when . . . the body releases a large amount of adrenaline into your system and you get what is referred to as a 'combat high.' This combat high is like getting an injection of morphine—you float around, laughing, joking, having a great time, totally oblivious to the dangers around you. . . . Problems arise when you begin to want another fix of combat, and another, and another, and, before you know it, you're hooked. As with heroin or cocaine addiction, combat addiction will surely get you killed. And like any addict, you get desperate and will do anything to get your fix."*[15]
>
> —*A Rhodesian combat veteran*

Several researchers report this "rush." Yet the subjects of the research had chronic PTSD, the reason for getting treatment. So this "rush" probably does not protect against getting PTSD, and might make it worse. As is common with "highs," a let-down follows.

A possible biological explanation is that with stress, the brain naturally releases opioids. For artificial drugs, these are related to morphine, heroin, and cocaine. Veterans' using those specific drugs as analogies is not coincidental. There is scientific speculation of an actual biochemical connection.

This can be applied across other groups. Some in occupations which involve killing may be ensnared in a situation not easy to leave, similar to the troubles addicts face while trying to stop taking drugs, for the same reason.

How ironic: A sense of euphoria can still be a reaction to trauma. Those brain-produced opioids are highly adaptive for those in danger, because they relieve extreme pain. When they are no longer adaptive but take over, it is a physical addiction. This may offer insight into the term "bloodthirsty."

PERPETRATION-INDUCED TRAUMATIC STRESS

There is yet much study to do, but current evidence indicates that killing tends to be traumatizing to at least some if not to most of those who do it—across the board of different kinds of killing.

There is a positive point to the idea that killing tends to make us sick: While psychologists some time ago debunked the proposition that humans have an instinct to kill, this evidence goes further.

It isn't merely that killing is not in our nature. It is *against* our nature.

NOTES AND REFERENCES

1. Tisdale, Sallie. October, 1987. We Do Abortions Here. *Harper's*, 66–70.

2. Johnson, Robert. 1998. *Death Work: A Study of the Modern Execution Process*. Belmont, CA: Wadsworth Publishing Company, p. 190.

3. Fanon, Frantz. 1968. *The Wretched of the Earth*. New York: Grove Press, Inc., p. 267.

4. Hendin, Herbert. 1997. *Seduced by Death: Doctors, Patients, and the Dutch Cure*. New York: W.W. Norton and Company, p. 52.

5. Such-Baer, Marianne. July 1974. Professional Staff Reaction to Abortion Work. *Social Casework*, 435–441.

6. Roe, Kathleen M. 1989. Private Troubles and Public Issues: Providing Abortion Amid Competing Definitions. *Social Science and Medicine*, 29, 1191–1198.

7. Glover, Hillel. 1988. Four Syndromes of Post-traumatic Stress Disorder: Stressors and Conflicts of the Traumatized with Special Focus on the Vietnam Combat Veteran. *Journal of Traumatic Stress*, 1, 57–78. Quote from p. 70.

8. Gianelli, Diane M. July 12, 1993. Abortion Providers Share Inner Conflicts. *American Medical News*.

9. Lifton, Robert J. 1990. Adult Dreaming: Frontiers of Form. In R. A. Neminoff & C. A. Colarusso, eds., *New Dimensions in Adult Development*. New York: Basic Books, pp. 419–442. Quote from p. 427.

10. Ibid., p. 429.

11. Haney, Craig. 2000. Reflections on the Stanford Prison Experiment: Genesis, Transformations, Consequences. In Thomas Blass, ed., *Obedience to Authority: Current Perspectives on the Milgram Paradigm*. Mahwah, NJ: Lawrence Erlbaum Associates, pp. 193–237. Quote from p. 226.

12. Trombley, Stephen. 1992. *The Execution Protocol: Inside America's Capital Punishment Industry*. New York: Crown Publishers, pp. 274–275; emphasis in original.

13. Johnson, *Death Work*, p. 181.

14. Solursh, Lionel P. 1988. Combat Addiction: Post-Traumatic Stress Disorder Re-explored. *Psychiatric Journal of the University of Ottawa*, 13, 17–20.

15. Grossman, Dave. 1995. *On Killing: The Psychological Cost of Learning to Kill in War and Society*. Boston: Little, Brown and Company, pp. 234–237.

Abortion and the Feminization of Poverty

Thomas W. Strahan

Connecting poverty to causing abortion is clear enough; material deprivation is one of the cruelest pressures to abort. Here Dr. Strahan suggests it also goes in the opposite direction: abortion increases poverty. War and racism cause poverty directly; abortion does so indirectly.

Since Dr. Strahan is now deceased, we offer excerpts from an article published in the journal Feminism & Nonviolence Studies *(http://www.fnsa.org/v1n3/strahan.html), originally published in 1994. Please refer to the same for more extensive references to the studies.*

The term "feminization of poverty" was first used by Diana Pearce when she observed that poverty seemed to be becoming more and more focused as a female problem. The phrase refers to the dramatic change in the composition of the poverty population in the United States in recent decades. Pearce noted that in 1976 almost two-thirds of the poor over 16 years of age were women and that this measure was growing, indicating that "it is women who account for an increasingly large portion of the economically disadvantaged."[1]

Until the 1960s, most poor families had husbands or other men present. Between 1969 and 1978, however, the number of poor families composed either of male only or husband and wife families dropped from 3.2 million to 2.6 million. During that same period, the number of poor families headed by women with minor children increased by one-third, from 1.8 to 2.7 million.[2]

This trend continued in the 1980s. . . .

This increased feminization of poverty coincides remarkably closely to the period of increasingly legalized abortion. Arguments have been made that the availability of abortion should help avoid this trend, because job loss due to childbirth would be avoided, as would the burdens of child care which so clearly contribute to povertization. The fact that the pattern has worsened precisely during the period when there was an upsurge in abortions suggests that, at the very least, abortion has been an inadequate solution to this poverty trend.

The causes of the feminization of poverty are varied and complex, as are any solutions.[3] However, experience suggests that, contrary to the above expectations, abortion may instead actually be a contributing factor. Through an increase in broken relationships, psychological difficulties, and substance abuse, a practice which is done exclusively on women may put them at greater economic disadvantage.

THE RAPID RISE OF REPEAT ABORTIONS

The abortion rate is much higher among the population of women who have already had at least one abortion. . . . Researchers have found that the socioeconomic status of women tends to deteriorate as abortion is repeated. In one study at Yale Medical School, researchers reviewed the records of the abortion clinic at Yale-New Haven Hospital of 886 women having a first or repeat abortion at the clinic during 1974–75. It was determined that women having first abortions were similar both in age and in years of completed education to those having repeat abortions. Women in the repeat abortion group were significantly more likely to be divorced (11.9% versus 6.1%), less likely to be a student (15.7% versus 27.7%), and more likely to be a welfare recipient (38.2% versus 25.8%). Among those repeating abortion, an average of approximately two years had elapsed since the previous abortion, but 42% had repeated abortions within the last 12 months.[4]

If unprotected sexual intercourse and "unwanted" pregnancy by women on welfare is considered undesirable, undergoing an induced abortion only heightens the problems.

BROKEN RELATIONSHIPS

Various studies have shown a weakening of social bonds (particularly with male partners) as abortion is increasingly utilized. As women have repeat abortions, their communications with others tend to break down. They tend more often to make the decision to abort by themselves. They are less likely to be happily married and tend to have more difficulty than other women in getting along with others. A Yale University study of 345 women at a New York abortion clinic found that women who have repeat abortions are in less stable social situations and have relationships of shorter duration than women who seek abortions for the first time.[5] The study also found that women having first abortions were generally more concerned with ethical issues, worry over the procedure itself, and the possibility of complications than were the women having repeat abortions. A study at the University of Pennsylvania found that repeat-abortion patients had more difficulty in getting along with others and evidenced significantly higher distress scores on interpersonal sensitivity, paranoid ideation, phobic anxiety, and sleep disturbance than women undergoing abortion for the first time.[6]

The trend for women who have abortions to undergo a deterioration of personal relationships, particularly with male partners, is of considerable importance economically. In the United States, for example, the median income of families in 1992 where there was a female householder with an absent husband was $18,587 compared to $42,140 for a married couple living together. Among households with children under 18 years of age, only 4.2% had an annual income of $10,000 or less if the children lived with both parents, compared to 42.7% if the children lived with the mother only.[7]

One of the many ways abortion can increase the likelihood of welfare status is by breaking up an existing relationship with a male partner. Evidence from a number of studies shows this to be the case. For example, in a study of 344 post-abortive women at the Akron Pregnancy Services Center in Akron, Ohio, during 1988–93, 49% reported that their relationship with the father of the unborn child ended soon after their abortion. Approximately six years after their abortion, only 22% were married, and 67% remained single.[8] Another study of women in a post-abortion support group at the Medical College of Ohio found that only 7 of the 66 women who had abortions while single eventually married the father.[9]

Abortion can also have a definite adverse effect on existing marriages which may lead to separation or divorce. This has been illustrated in the medical literature and elsewhere.[10] . . .

The fact that the abortion also means that there is not a child whose care requires expense does not necessarily change the situation, because replacement pregnancies are common. A study of Chicago adolescents, for example, demonstrated a tendency to conceive again shortly after an induced abortion, miscarriage or other loss of a fetus or infant.[11]

PSYCHOLOGICAL DIFFICULTIES

The psychological stability required to work one's way out of an impoverished state is also impaired by abortion, especially repeated abortions. Evidence of denial and isolation is frequently observed among women who repeat abortion. By way of illustration, one researcher who favors the legality of abortion described an interview with a 16-year-old who said she had just had her second abortion, although her Planned Parenthood counselor said it was her fourth: "This abortion doesn't make me feel sad, I feel good.... There are no complications and Medicaid pays for it.... Being Catholic doesn't bother me at all. But I don't confess it. I'm scared of what the priest would say. I wish I could tell my mother. But she would be so angry."[12] This girl believes she is in charge of her own behavior, but denial and impaired communication with important people in her life are obvious problems.

Masochism or self-punishment has been identified as a factor in repeat abortions; from that same researcher comes the case of a professional who had undergone three abortions. "I hated myself. I felt abandoned and lost... And I felt guilty about killing something. I couldn't get it out of my head that I'd just killed a baby."[13] A 30-year-old single woman recalled: "I was totally irresponsible about birth control. It was like I was just wanting to be punished.... I didn't go out to do it, but I didn't do anything not to make it happen."[14] These illustrative cases do not come from an anti-abortion bias, since the researcher reporting them is of the opposite opinion.

The well-documented fact that lower-income people are more likely to be philosophically opposed to abortion than those of higher income also means that those who do abort are emotionally harder hit. A study by researcher Larry Peppers of Clemons University on a group of women who had abortions at an Atlanta hospital found that those who had abortions for financial reasons were among the group with the highest post-abortion grief reactions.[15]

SUBSTANCE ABUSE

The women with a history of abortion also had increasingly higher smoking levels as the number of prior abortions increased.[16] The increasing smoking rates among women as abortion is repeated has other possible side effects that would not ordinarily be assumed. Studies have shown that smokers are less likely than non-smokers to use contraceptives or plan a pregnancy.[17]

More troubling for an analysis of what causes increased poverty in women would be abuse of alcohol and illicit drugs. Despite the report of the World Health Organization in 1975 that women who have undergone induced abortion tend to consume alcohol more than the general population,[18] there has been no systematic study of the problem. However, based on various studies and anecdotal reports, it appears that the elevated use of alcohol as well as other drugs stems, in large part, from the effects of the abortion experience itself.

Alcohol and drug abuse following induced abortion has a potential increased risk for women in a variety of health and social aspects. Alcohol impairs the immune system and puts a woman at risk for a variety of diseases. Social deterioration may occur due to sexual dysfunction, increased violence, hospitalization, job loss, increased isolation, self-destructive behavior, and poverty status. Maternal health and the well-being of offspring may be impaired due to alcohol or drug use during subsequent pregnancies, including low birth weight, miscarriages, fetal alcohol syndrome, congenital malformation or perinatal mortality.[19] Additionally, subsequent children may have greater learning difficulties.[20] The connection of all these problems to a greater feminization of poverty requires little imagination.

CAUSE AND EFFECT

The many studies that show a correlation between abortion, especially repeated abortions, and a reduction in women's economic well-being do not, for the most part, prove a clear causation. While anecdotal evidence may support the contention that abortion increases the breakup of relationships, psychological difficulties, and substance abuse, the argument can be and has been made that the causation is in the other direction. Those women inclined toward multiple abortions are also inclined to have these problems. More precisely, the same thing that is causing these women to have these problems may also be causing the multiple abortions. It is not that the abortions cause the difficulties, but that problems with unhealthy sexual relations with men, domestic violence, and similar challenges may cause both the abortions and the subsequent problems that are correlated with them. This argument is frequently used by abortion counselors and promoters.

However, another causal factor must be taken into account: to what extent does the ready accessibility of abortion cause the problems of exploitational sexual attitudes and self-righteous denials of responsibility by men? To what extent does the presence of the abortion clinic itself exacerbate the problems that cause both the abortions and the subsequent psychological difficulties?

In any event, the very least that can be said from this evidence is that repeated abortion is not therapeutic. The repeated utilization of abortion does not appear to lead to economic prosperity or social well-being. The argument that abortion accessibility is necessary to help eradicate poverty cannot be maintained in the face of the evidence.

More probably, the practice of abortion is leading to greater impoverishment of women. Abortion is a practice aimed at women, and therefore any impoverishing effects as described above would disproportionately impact on women. When we know that current trends involve a "feminization of poverty," any possible factor that exacerbates the problem should be examined. There is ample evidence to suggest that the widespread use of abortion is such a factor, which should, despite political ideologies, receive greater scrutiny.

NOTES AND REFERENCES

1. Pearce, Diana. February 1978. The Feminization of Poverty: Women, Work, and Welfare," *Urban and Social Change Review, 12*, 30.

2. Blaustein, Arthur. 1982. *The American Promise*. New Brunswick, NJ: Transaction Books, p. 8.

3. See, for example, Northrop, Emily M. March 1990. The Feminization of Poverty: The Demographic Factor and the Composition of Economic Growth. *Journal of Economic Issues, 24*(1), 145.

4. Shepard, Mary Jo & Michael B. Bracken. 1979. Contraceptive Practice and Repeat Induced Abortion: An Epidemiological Investigation. *Journal of Biosocial Science, 11*, 289–302.

5. Bracken Michael B. & Stanislav K. Kasl. 1975. First and Repeat Abortions: A Study of Decision-Making and Delay. *Journal of Biosocial Science, 7*, 374–491.

6. Freeman, Ellen. May, 1980. Emotional Distress Patterns among Women Having First or Repeat Abortions. *Obstetrics and Gynecology*, 55(5), 630.

7. *Statistical Abstracts of the United States*. 1994. U.S. Department of Commerce, Bureau of the Census.

8. Gsellman, Lee Ellen. September/October 1993. Physical and Psychological Injury in Women Following Abortion: Akron Pregnancy Services Survey. *Association for Interdisciplinary Research Newsletter*, 5(4), 1–8.

9. Franco, Kathleen N., Marijo B. Tamburrino, & Nancy B. Campbell. 1989. Psychological Profile of Dysphoric Women Post-Abortion. *Journal of the American Medical Women's Association*, 44(113), 113–115.

10. See, for example, Moore, Christopher R. October 14, 1991. Husband Mourns Outcome of Wife's Painful Decision. *American Medical News*, 24; Strahan, Thomas.

November/December 1991. Portraits of Post-Abortive Fathers Devastated by the Abortion Experience. *Association for Interdisciplinary Research Newsletter*, 7(3), 1–8.
11. Horowitz, Nancy Heller. November, 1978. Adolescent Mourning Reactions to Infant and Fetal Loss. *Social Casework*, 59, 551–559.
12. Francke, Linda. 1978. *The Ambivalence of Abortion*. New York: Random House, pp. 190–191.
13. Ibid., p. 61.
14. Ibid., p. 65.
15. Peppers, Larry G. 1989. Grief and Elective Abortion: Implications for the Counselor. In Kenneth J. Doka, *Disenfranchised Grief, Recognizing Hidden Sorrow*. Lexington, MA: Lexington Books, pp. 135–146.
16. Mandelson, Margaret T., Christopher B. Maden, & Janet R. Daling. March, 1992. Low Birth Weight in Relation to Multiple Induced Abortions. *American Journal of Public Health*, 82(3), 391.
17. Yerushalmy, J. 1971. The Relationship of Parents' Cigarette Smoking to the Outcome of Pregnancy. *American Journal of Epidemiology*, 93(6), 443.
18. Harlap, Susan & Michael Davies. 1975. Characteristics of Pregnant Women Reporting Previous Induced Abortions. *Bulletin of the World Health Organization*, 52, 49; Gestation, Birth-Weight and Spontaneous Abortion in Pregnancy after Induced Abortion: Report of the Collaborative Study by the World Health Organization Task Force on Sequelae of Abortion. (1975, January 20). *The Lancet*, 142–145.
19. Food and Drug Administration Drug Bulletin. 1981. Surgeon General's Advisory on Alcohol and Pregnancy. *Department of Health and Human Services*, 11(2), 9–10.
20. Newman, Lucille & Stephen L. Buka. 1990. Every Child a Learner: Reducing Risks of Learning Impairment during Pregnancy and Infancy. Education Commission of the States, Denver, CO.

7

The Direct Killing of Racism and Poverty

Poverty can kill people, and the connection of racism to poverty is well established. When people die as a result of the way things are set up, as opposed to being directly targeted, it is called "structural violence."

Yet, people can also be directly targeted, with lynching and mob violence. If lynching were still socially approved, it would be one of the major advocacy issues of the consistent life ethic. It's a sign of progress that it now gets more universal social condemnation.

Wars with racist motivation have the same effect on a larger scale. Racism in the treatment of a government's own soldiers can also lead to casualties. When pressures are brought to die deliberately in assisted suicide and euthanasia, it stands to reason that those who are traditionally targeted for discrimination will be targeted here as well. We may tragically find this more if the practice became more widespread or open and countable.

We have much more detail on how abortion and the death penalty are ways by which racism and poverty literally lead to a dead end. In this chapter, we use a variety of sources to illustrate the point.

ABORTION

Erma Clardy Craven[I]

It takes little imagination to see that the unborn Black baby is the real object of many abortionists. Except for the privilege of aborting herself, the Black woman and her family must fight for every other social and economic privilege. This move toward the free application of a non-right (abortion) for those whose real need is equal human rights and opportunities is benumbing the social conscience of America into unquestioningly accepting the "smoke screen" of abortion. The quality of life for the poor, the Black and the oppressed will not be served by destroying their children.

Edward Allred, millionaire abortionist[2]

When a sullen black woman of 17 or 18 can decide to have a baby and get welfare and food stamps and become a burden to us all, it's time to stop. In parts of South Los Angeles, having babies for welfare is the only industry the people have.

and

Population control is too important to be stopped by some right wing pro-life types. Take the new influx of Hispanic immigrants. Their lack of respect for democracy and social order is frightening. I hope I can do something to stem that tide; I'd set up a clinic in Mexico for free if I could.

Fatimah Shabbaz[3]

At first, I was pro-choice too. However, a racial incident that occurred in 1971 made it clear to me that the practice of abortions on demand is a direct threat to the future existence of Black America.

In 1971, my husband and I were poor struggling college students. Therefore, I was forced to rely on the Cincinnati Public Health Department for my pre-natal care.

One day, the white clinic social worker invited me into her office for what amounted to a family-values/pro-life pep talk. She spoke about the need to maintain our "respect for life" in the face of poverty and hardship.

I took this to be a kind gesture of encouragement, until I returned to the clinic for my next appointment. This same white social worker walked over to the black expectant mother who was sitting next to me. Then she asked the young woman in clear earshot of everyone, "Have you considered getting an abortion?"

For a moment I was totally puzzled. It was hard to believe that this was the same person who spoke to me privately a month earlier.

Then I looked at my clinic data card and noticed *that someone had mistakenly listed my race as white!* (You could not necessarily recognize the mistake just by looking at me. The other pregnant mother was more visibly black, of course.)

In the 1990's, government-sponsored health care is still dominated by affluent white health care professionals who administer to the poor. The African-American community does *not* control the public health care system today, not even in communities that are predominantly black.

Common sense should tell us that this condition of inequality is dangerous for African-Americans when it comes to the debate over "reproductive rights," an issue which will ultimately determine which people in society will live or die. This debate will determine the limits on government officials whose policy decisions are now a matter of life or death in reference to the poor, the unborn, the elderly, and the terminally ill!

Pro-choicers have convinced the public that legalized abortions are an act of mercy toward low-income mothers. They argue that government-funded abortions need to be more accessible to the poor. However, this kind of argument defies all reason, if you really think about it. The whole idea that poverty is an acceptable reason for the murder of unborn babies has had a devastating impact on the African-American community.

Elizabeth Liagin[4]

One of the most revealing clues as to the intentions of western foreign policy planners is that population literature intended for public consumption . . . nearly *always* makes reference to food shortages, depleted natural resources, environmental degradation, and overcrowding. Documents intended only for *internal* consumption, on the other hand, almost *never* focus on this type of argument. For instance, a top secret memorandum of the now-defunct Operations Coordinating Board of the National Security Council with the heading "Outline Plan of Operations for Latin America" expresses the consternation of U.S. leaders about population change: "The rapid rate of population increase and economic growth in the area, with their *implications for probable future strength and importance to the United States*, should be taken into consideration in the execution of all programs."[5] In other words, the economic growth that accompanies population increase, rather than the disadvantages that contemporary population policy propaganda portrays, is what Washington views as the real threat to its objectives in Latin America. This theme permeates throughout the archives of U.S. foreign affairs with reference to every developing region.

A more recent example of the same thinking regarding Latin America appears in a 1991 research paper prepared for the US Army Conference on Long-Range Planning: "Though the populations of the nine Asian countries in the sample more than tripled during this period, and the population of the six Latin American countries rose by a factor of nearly seven, per capita output is estimated to have risen dramatically as well—by a factor of more than three for the Asian group and by nearly five for the Latin American group . . . Evidently, rapid population growth has not prevented major improvements in productivity in many of the societies most directly transformed by it."[6]

This is a critical revelation. *Per capita* income in the Latin American countries under study—the ratio of money to people—increased five-fold during a period when population increased by a factor of nearly seven. This means that overall gross earnings in the region would have increased *35-fold* during the period, each person, on the average, gained by a multiple of five, and there were seven times as many people. This does not suggest the economic stagnation predicted by western policy propaganda, but rather a dramatic growth in regional wealth and prestige.

If all the rhetoric about population growth *impeding* development were truly believed in Washington, the "benevolent" U.S. policy-makers would be delighted that the Latin American nations have done so well, saving the U S. millions, perhaps billions, in poverty-preventing contraceptive [and abortion] programs, but the record shows no sense of relief: "The population and economic-growth trends described could create an international environment even more menacing to the security prospects of the Western alliance than was the Cold War for the past generation."[7]

Clearly, there is no other issue that incites a sense of crisis in western policy-makers comparable to the matter of population growth in the developing world. And no other matter intersects with virtually every element of international power: access to materials for military use, projected troop strength, relative economic advantage, political domination, racial potency, and cultural influences.

DEATH PENALTY

Sr. Helen Prejean[8]

I don't believe the death penalty is a peripheral issue of morality for our culture. It is connected to three deep wounds of our society, wounds which must be healed.

One wound is racism. Nowhere do you see racial inequalities more than in the punishments we give for crimes. The second wound is our treatment of those who are poor. Although less than one percent of the people who commit homicide end up on death row, everyone who receives the death penalty is poor. The third is our penchant for violence as a solution to our social problems. Our government kills to show that killing is wrong.

The death penalty is intimately connected with each of these larger social problems. To move toward healing, we must address these realities that surround society's support of capital punishment.

I became a sister [nun] in 1957 and began teaching in White suburban parishes. For years I prayed for the poor, for justice—but I had no connection to the lives of those in poverty. But one night one of our sisters, Marie Augusta Neal, said something I will never forget: "Jesus preached good news to the poor," she said. "Integral to that good news was that they would be poor no longer."

Those words shifted the axis of my spiritual life . . . I had to be on the side of poor people. And I knew I couldn't simply pray for poor folk, yet live apart from them. I had to embrace their struggles. That year, I moved into the St. Thomas housing projects in New Orleans.

I learned things at St. Thomas that I never could have learned elsewhere. Outside my window, drugs were as common as loaves of bread. When I complained to the mayor's office, they responded, "Every city has its problems. At least we know where they are." City officials seemed to feel that Black kids in St. Thomas could drown in drugs as long as those drugs didn't plague other neighborhoods.

When residents of St. Thomas were killed, if there was any newspaper coverage, it was a tiny story on page fourteen. When White people were killed, it was front-page news.

Supreme Court Cases

In 1987, lawyers for death row inmate Warren McCleskey presented a rigorous statistical analysis of Georgia's sentencing procedures. With a study of over 2,000 cases, after accounting for around 200 variables including previous criminal record, the conclusion was that the odds of a death sentence when blacks killed whites were about eleven times higher than the reverse.

The Supreme Court accepted the validity of most of the study's findings but added, "Apparent disparities in sentencing are an inevitable part of our criminal justice system." In a 5–4 opinion written by Justice Lewis Powell, the statistical proof of bias was not grounds to reverse a sentence or to invalidate the state's sentencing procedures. This means the burden is on the defendant to prove that prejudice impacted the sentencing in his or her individual case. Since racial bias is rarely admitted, burden of proof is practically impossible.

Several years later, Justice Powell admitted that he had not fully understood the statistical evidence of prejudice in the McClesky case and wished he had voted differently. He said, "I have come to think that capital punishment should be abolished."

NOTES AND REFERENCES

1. Hilgers, Thomas W. & Dennis J. Horan, eds. 1972. *Abortion and Social Justice.* New York: Sheed & Ward.

2. Doctor's Abortion Business Is Lucrative, *San Diego Union*, October 12, 1980, p. B-1.

3. A Case of Mistaken Identity, http://www.pregnantpause.org/racism/mistaken.htm (accessed on December 19, 2007).

4. Liagin, Elizabeth. 1996. Excessive Force: Power, Politics & Population Control. Information Project for Africa, pp. 115–122. Excerpt edited for conciseness.

5. Operations Coordinating Board. January 1957. Outline Plan of Operations for Latin America, p. 3.

6. U.S. Army Conference on Long Range Planning. Summer, 1991. Population Change and National Security. *Foreign Affairs*, 70(3), 117.

7. Ibid., pp. 128–129.

8. The Death Penalty. *The Other Side* magazine, http://www.theotherside.org/archive/sep-dec97/prejean.html (accessed July 17, 2006).

When Bigotry Turns Disabilities Deadly

People with disabilities are the one group to which most of us belong. Most people have a mild disability, like dentures or eyeglasses. Most of us will have a more severe disability for a period, through an accident or illness or surgery. However, those people whose disabilities are above average in severity or permanence may have to face the burden of narrow-mindedness from others. This injustice becomes especially vicious when used for death-dealing.

People are not required to have the virtues or satisfactions we offer below to have their lives valued—being a living human being is enough. Yet there are still inaccurate impressions on disability to be corrected.

Even unconscious people, who do not have anything on that list, offer us an extremely valuable service. As long as their lives are protected, people seen as most on the margins, then the rest of us are safe. Those on the edge of the social fabric guard it and keep it from unraveling. The first step on the slippery slope is not taken, so there is no slippery slide.

THE VALUE OF LIFE WITH A DISABILITY

(adapted from Not Dead Yet at http://www.notdeadyet.org/docs/value.html)

We are a vital and proud community, with values that enhance our quality of life and could enhance life for all:

1. tolerance for others' differences (racial, intellectual, financial)
2. matter-of-fact orientation toward helping; acceptance of human interdependence

3. high tolerance for unknowns or less-than-ideal outcomes
4. characteristic dark humor, laughing at the oppressor, finding humor everywhere
5. highly developed skills at managing multiple problems, systems, and helpers
6. creativity, lack of rigidity, ability to use new ways to solve problems
7. sophisticated future orientation; planning around anticipated obstacles
8. ability to read others' attitudes; skill at filling in the gaps and sorting out contradictory messages

RESEARCH ON "QUALITY OF LIFE"

(adapted from Not Dead Yet at http://www.notdeadyet.org/docs/disqual.html)

- Of spinal cord injured high-level quadriplegics, 86% rated their quality of life as average or better. Only 17% of their medical staff thought they could have an average or better quality of life (KA Gerhart et al., *Annals of Emergency Medicine*, 1994, vol. 23, 807–812).
- No differences were found between 190 physically disabled persons and 195 "able- bodied" persons on ratings of life satisfaction, frustration with life or mood (P Cameron et al., *Journal of Consulting and Clinical Psychology*, 1973, vol. 41, 207–214).
- A disability's duration was positively related to accepting disability in persons with spinal-cord injury-related paralysis. Severity of disability was not important in accepting life with a disability (F Woodrich & JB Patterson, *Journal of Rehabilitation*, 1983, July–Sept., 26–30).
- Of paraplegics, 60% reported feelings more positively about themselves since becoming disabled (C Ray & J West, *Paraplegia*, 1984, vol. 22, 75–86).
- Interviews and tests of 133 persons with severe mobility disabilities revealed no differences between them and the nondisabled norm on psychosocial measures. In another study, no significant difference was found between persons with severe disabilities and persons with no disabilities on quality-of-life measures (R Stensman, *Scandinavian Journal of Rehabilitation Medicine*, 1985, vol. 17, 87–99).
- In a study of life satisfaction of quadriplegics, fewer than a third of those using ventilators expressed dissatisfaction with their lives. Evidence shows life satisfaction scores are higher in persons who have had more time to adjust to disability (JR Bach & MC Tilton, *Archives of Physical Medicine and Rehabilitation*, 1994, vol. 75, 626–632).

- Spinal-cord injured rehabilitation patients were similar to the general population on self-ratings of depression, yet hospital staff consistently overestimated patients' level of depression (LA Cushman & MP Dijkers, *Archives of Physical Medicine and Rehabilitation*, 1990, vol. 71, 191–196).
- Three-quarters of persons with spinal-cord injuries rated their quality of life as good or excellent. Amount of paralysis made no difference, but people using ventilators rated their quality of life higher than those not needing ventilators (GG Whiteneck et al., *Rocky Mountain Spinal Cord Injury System Report to the National Institute of Handicapped Research*, 1985, 29–33).

DISABILITY RIGHTS CONNECTED TO ISSUES OF VIOLENCE

(Scott Rains)

Scott Rains served for several years as co-coordinator of the pioneering consistent ethic group Prolifers for Survival. This article originally appeared in their newsletter in the 1980s.

Why would a person with a disability get involved in peace or prolife work? What might they have that was unique to offer?

A disability is not something that happens in a vacuum, but to a person. It may dramatically change the course of a person's life or color it from birth, but it is no more than an overlay, a part of one's personality, and it can be used like a lens to look at one's place in society.

So, while it isn't possible to generalize about "the disabled" meaningfully, it is helpful to look at what the experience of being a person with a disability might do to one's perception. Similar reflection by other minority groups has generated, for instance, the women's movement and the civil right movement.

Liberation movements operate on the truth that no one can ultimately win freedom for someone else. The oppressed must take up their own struggle for freedom and in the process reach out in coalition with others. In the prolife movement an example might be Women Exploited by Abortion, who represent one group of the victims of abortion. But the unborn, by their nature, are unable to start their own liberation movement.

My own decision to become publicly active in the prolife movement was, I admit, rather selfish. I followed the news stories while a newborn child was starved at an Indiana hospital because he was born with Downs syndrome. The years I had spent fighting for federal architectural standards, for equal access and equal employment suddenly didn't make sense. If the new strategy was to eliminate those of us with disabilities at birth, then that was where I would stand up for our rights.

It wasn't sentimentality or a moral judgment about the inherent quality of every human life that motivated me. It was solidarity. Having looked at the world with the perspective of a man with a physical disability, I saw an attitude—and a mechanism—of oppression, as tangible as racism, that held people like myself at the margins of society. Soon many other disabled activists saw the connection and a flurry of legislative action on infanticide followed.

If being open to the experience of one's disability can lead to action in the prolife movement, what about in the peace movement? A disabled veteran of Vietnam is not likely to have a romanticized idea of war. The disabled children of hibakusha (survivors of Hiroshima and Nagasaki) don't need to ask if it is a sin to build nuclear weapons. During the United Nations' International Year of the Disabled Person, students at one college showed a film on the nuclear destruction of Hiroshima under the theme "Prevent Disabilities/Prevents War."

The peace movement is characterized by coalitions. Respecting the experience of others in the coalition leads to a more complete understanding of the process of building peace. It wasn't that long ago that the deaf community was not visible in peace work. Now American Sign Language interpreters share the stage with speakers and performers. A more inclusive movement models to society the things that make for peace. It also puts a human face on the costs of preparing for war. Bringing "Star Wars" down to earth is not hard for someone on Social Security or Veteran's Disability Benefits. It is as close as the inadequate monthly check.

Sometimes the disability itself takes on an almost symbolic meaning—or to put it another way, it becomes a "media event." I can think of several examples from my own experience.

Once as 493 of us approached the gate of a nuclear weapons site to trespass, accompanied by several hundred supporters, the tension on both sides of the fence began to rise. The plan was to climb over the fence. My situation called for a different solution. I negotiated futilely for some time with the MP sergeant to open the gate. I wanted to come in and get arrested (too).

Then I came on a plan. At the comer of the gate was a gutter just deep enough for me to squeeze under the fence. When the sergeant turned his back, I slipped from my wheelchair to the ground and under the fence.

Immediately, several MP's rushed over to me—not to arrest me, but to bring me my wheelchair and see that I was all right. The tension was broken.

What had been building into a confrontation resolved into compassion and understanding.

Another time I was on a televised debate. My opponent was the state director of the Religious Coalition for Abortion Rights. Her presentation was smooth (even when her facts were wrong), but she pushed her innuendo a little too far. Discussing "quality of life" as a criterion for choosing abortion, it became clear that neither I nor my people met her definition of "quality." The sermon that I spontaneously delivered to this person who presumed the ability to judge the quality of my life was of the fire-and-brimstone variety. But there was no pulpit more fitting to deliver it from than where I was sitting—in my wheelchair.

A disability does not confer special knowledge on a person, but it can become an impetus for reflection on things not generally perceived. It can lead a person with the disability to associate with others in a similar situation and develop a sense of community and a desire to take responsibility in society. It can provide the opportunity for others to reflect on their own needs and to be moved to respond to the needs of those around them. It can also give us a glimpse of the waste that is war and the beauty that is hidden in each new life conceived.

Right to Life of Humans and Animals

Vasu Murti

> *"The reasons for legal intervention in favor of children apply not less strongly to the case of those unfortunate slaves—the animals."*[1]
>
> —*John Stuart Mill*

Animals are highly complex creatures, possessing a brain, central nervous system, and sophisticated mental life. Animals *suffer* at the hands of their human tormentors.

We know the feminist movement originally opposed abortion as "child-murder" (Susan B. Anthony's words) and a form of violence women are forced into in a patriarchal society with inadequate concern or respect for new mothers.[2] Many of the early American feminists—including Lucy Stone, Amelia Bloomer, Susan B. Anthony, and Elizabeth Cady Stanton—were also connected with the nineteenth-century animal welfare movement. Together, they would meet with antislavery editor Horace Greeley to toast "Women's Rights and Vegetarianism."[3]

Many early American feminists saw animal rights as the logical next step in social progress after women's rights and civil rights. Count Leo Tolstoy similarly described ethical vegetarianism as social progress:

> And there are ideas of the future, of which some are already approaching realization and are obliging people to change their way of life and to struggle against the former ways: such ideas in our world as those of freeing the laborers, of giving equality to women, of ceasing to use flesh-food, and so on.[4]

The case for animal rights and vegetarianism should be readily understandable to the millions of Americans opposed to abortion on demand. Pro-life activist Karen Swallow Prior writes,

> Although I may disagree with some of its underlying principles there is much for me, an anti-abortion activist, to respect in the animal rights movement. Animal rights activists, like me, have risked personal safety and reputation for the sake of other living beings. Animal rights activists, like me, are viewed by many in the mainstream as fanatical wackos, ironically exhorted by irritated passerby to "Get a Life!"
>
> Animal rights activists, like me, place a higher value on life than on personal comfort and convenience, and in balancing the sometimes competing interests of rights and responsibilities, choose to err on the side of compassion and nonviolence.[5]

Both the antiabortion and animal rights movements consider their cause a form of social progress, like abolition of human slavery or emancipation of women. Leaders in both movements have even compared themselves to abolitionists who sought to end human slavery. Dr. J.C. Willke, former head of National Right to Life, wrote a book titled *Abortion and Slavery*. Like abortion opponents drawing a parallel between the *Dred Scott* decision and *Roe v. Wade*, Dr. Tom Regan also draws a parallel between human and animal slavery in *The Case for Animal Rights*.

Both movements see themselves extending human rights to an excluded class of beings. Both claim to speak on behalf of members of a minority group unable to defend themselves from oppression. Both compare the mass destruction to the Nazi Holocaust.

Feminist writer Carol J. Adams notes the parallels between the two movements: "A woman attempts to enter a building. Others, massed outside, try to thwart her attempt. They shout at her, physically block her way, frantically call her names, pleading with her to respect life. Is she buying a fur coat or getting an abortion?"[6]

The Fur Information Council of America asks, "If fashion isn't about freedom of choice, what is? Personal choice is not just a fur industry issue. It's everybody's issue."[7] Like the abortion debate, lines are drawn. "Freedom of choice" vs. taking an innocent life. "Personal lifestyle" vs. violating another's rights.

Animal rights activists have even proven to be "antichoice," depending upon the issue. A letter in *The Animals' Voice Magazine* states,

> Exit polls in Aspen, Colorado, after the failed 1989 fur ban was voted on, found that most people were against fur but wanted people to have a choice to wear it. Instead of giving in, we should take the offensive and state in no uncertain terms that to abuse and kill animals is wrong, period! There is no choice because another being had to suffer to produce that item . . . an eventual ban on fur would be impossible if we tell people that they have some sort of "choice" to kill . . . remember, no one has the right to choose death over life for another being.[8]

A letter in *Veg-News* read,

> I did have some concerns about [the] Veg Psych column which asserted that we must respect a non-vegan's "right to choose" her/his food. While I would never advocate intolerance (quite the opposite actually), arguing that we have a "right to choose" when it comes to eating meat, eggs, and dairy is akin to saying we have a "right to choose" to beat dogs, harass wildlife, and torture cats. . . . Clearly, we have the ability to choose to cause animal abuse, but that doesn't translate into a right to make that choice.[9]

Recognizing rights in another class of beings naturally limits our freedoms and choices, requiring a change in personal lifestyle. The abolition of (human) slavery is a good example. Both movements appear to be imposing their own personal moral convictions upon the rest of our secular society.

Animal rights activists document health hazards of meat and dairy products,[10] while antiabortion activists educate about the link between abortion and breast cancer.[11] "Overpopulation" frequently justifies abortion as birth control. On a vegetarian diet, however, the world could easily support a population several times its present size. The world's cattle alone consume enough to feed 8.7 billion humans.[12] Both movements make use of graphic photos or videos of abortion victims or tortured animals. Both movements speak of respecting life and of compassion.

Both movements cite studies that demonstrate that violence toward an oppressed class of beings leads to worse forms of violence in human society, known as the "slippery slope." The term was coined by Malcolm Muggeridge, a pro-life vegetarian. For example, since abortion was legalized, child abuse rates have risen dramatically. Acceptance of abortion, activists argue, leads to a devaluation of human life and paves the way toward acceptance of infanticide and euthanasia. Animal rights activists likewise compare the lives of animals to those of human children—brutality to animals brutalizes humans into insensitivity toward one another.

A Soviet study found that over 87 percent of a group of violent criminals had, as children, burned, hanged or stabbed domestic animals, and an American study at Yale found that children who abuse animals have a much higher likelihood of becoming violent criminals.[13] Most recent studies show a strong connection between children being cruel to pets as a pattern building up to a pattern of violence against other human beings. The evidence is mounting.[14] Even the U.S. Federal Bureau of Investigation has said, "investigation and prosecution of crimes against animals is an important tool for identifying people who are, or may become, perpetrators of violent crimes against people."[15]

Pro-lifers have reason to be especially concerned about violence toward animals. Animals are sentient beings possessing many mental capacities comparable to those of young human children. If we fail to see them as part of our moral community, how will we ever embrace humans in their most primitive stages of development? Antiabortionists are horrified as a class of humans are systematically stripped of rights, executed, and even used in medical research. Yet we humans have done this to animals for millennia.

C.S. Lewis and other people of faith have acknowledged that denying rights to animals merely because they lack the same level of rational thought most humans exhibit at full development means also denying rights to the mentally handicapped, the senile, and other classes of humans.[16] Herein lies the basis for better understanding and cooperation between two movements seeking liberty and justice for all.

NOTES AND REFERENCES

1. Williams, Howard. 1883. *The Ethics of Diet.* London: F. Pitman.

2. Derr, Mary Krane, MacNair, Rachel, Naranjo-Huebl, Linda. 2006. *ProLife Feminism: Yesterday and Today,* 2nd ed. Philadelphia, PA: Xlibris.

3. Singer, Peter. 1975. *Animal Liberation.* New York: Avon Books.

4. Giehl, Dudley. 1979. *Vegetarianism: A Way of Life.* New York: Harper & Row, p. 132.

5. Animal Rights Activists Somehow Have Mixed Feelings When It Comes to Abortion. *Buffalo News,* June 4, 1996 (Buffalo, NY).

6. Adams, Carol J. 1991. Abortion Rights and Animal Rights. *Feminists for Animal Rights,* 6(1/2), 1.

7. Ibid., p. 1.

8. Goodwin, J. P. 1994. What More You Can Do to Fight Fur. *The Animals' Voice Magazine,* 7(2), 7.

9. Norris, Jack. 2003. Letter to the Editor. *Veg-News* (San Francisco, CA).

10. See, for example, Web site of Physician's Committee for Responsible Medicine: http://www.pcrm.org.

11. See, for example, http://www.abortionbreastcancer.com.
12. Akers, Keith. 1986. *A Vegetarian Sourcebook.* Arlington, VA: Vegetarian Press, p. 94.
13. Robbins, John. 1987. *Diet for a New America.* Walpole, NH: Stillpoint Publishing, p. 23.
14. Two sources that document this are Miller, C. 2001. Childhood Animal Cruelty and Interpersonal Violence. *Clinical Psychology Review, 21,* 735–749, and Merz-Perez, Linda and Kathleen M. Heide. (2004). *Animal Cruelty: Pathway to Violence Against People.* Walnut Creek, CA: AltaMira Press.
15. Lockwood, R. and A. Church. 1998. Deadly Serious: An FBI Perspective on Animal Cruelty. In R. Lockwood and F. A. Ascione, eds., *Cruelty to Animals and Interpersonal Violence.* West Lafayette, IN: Purdue University Press, pp. 241–246.
16. Linzey, Andrew and Tom Regan, eds. 1989. *Animals and Christianity.* New York: Crossroad Publishing Company, pp. 63–64.

10

Does the Seamless Garment Fit? American Public Opinion

Edith Bogue

In 1983, when Joseph Cardinal Bernardin first articulated a "consistent ethic of life," he spoke neither as a social activist nor as a social scientist. Rather, he drew together threads from philosophy and theology, weaving an ideology that was soon known as the *seamless garment of life*. Its fundamental principle was not new. What was utterly unique was the simultaneous application of Albert Schweitzer's touchstone value of *respect for life* to so many disparate social situations: care for the incurably or terminally ill, women considering abortion, prisoners facing the death penalty, war and military spending, and a growing gap between the rich and poor. Each of these issues can be—and had been—carefully studied and explored in its own context; Bernardin drew them into a single, unified whole. His approach has been developed by proponents within and beyond the Catholic Church and widely debated; it continues to shape the thinking and discourse in many life-issue debates. After such an extended examination, it is fair to ask: is the seamless garment a good fit for the attitudes and perspectives of the American public?

The last quarter of the twentieth century witnessed the emergence of a multiplicity of issues each related to respect for life. A pastoral letter disputing the morality of nuclear weapons, *The Challenge of Peace*, provided the stimulus for Bernardin's profound study of pro-life theology. The rapid pace of social and technological change produced an ever-shifting context in which respect-for-life issues were debated. Medicine's growing ability to maintain human life confronted patients and families with the difficult decision of whether or when to decline extended medical treatment or terminate sophisticated life-support systems. Dr. Jack Kevorkian, popularly known as Dr. Death, openly assisted over hundred patients in committing suicide, actions that sparked legislation both to legalize and to criminalize assisted suicide.

After the U.S. Supreme Court overturned state laws against abortion in 1973, the number of legal abortion performed greatly increased, from just over 600,000 in 1973 to a peak of 1.4 million in 1990. Abortion facilities have become an integral part of the nation's health care system, at least in densely populated parts of the country.[1] The development of morning-after pills and the advent of chemically induced abortions through RU-486 privatized the procedure and expanded the range of arguments on all sides of the debate.

The death penalty was suspended in the United States in 1972 when the Supreme Court ruled, in *Furman v. Georgia,* that it was arbitrarily, even "freakishly" applied, and therefore constituted cruel and unusual punishment. When the Court allowed it again, the majority of states quickly reinstated capital punishment; Gary Gilmore's 1976 execution by a firing squad inaugurated the "modern era" of the death penalty. Lethal injection was first used as a more "humane" and less violent method of capital punishment in 1982. The number of executions climbed from one or two per year to ninety-eight in 1999. DNA testing and other forensic advances revealed the presence of innocent people on death row. Some states called a moratorium on executions to investigate their criminal justice systems. Yet high-tech forensics enabled some jurors to feel more confident in convicting and sentencing someone to death.

Widely divergent views of the causes of poverty and impact of welfare resulted in waves of "welfare reform" as the gap between rich and poor widened. Changing family structures and a spike in divorce rates were blamed by some, the transformation of the workforce in a globalized economy by others. An ethos of self-sufficiency came to dominate programs that provided aid to the poor, and the pledge to "end welfare as we know it" gained popular support.

It is difficult, now, to remember the intensity of debate about nuclear arms as the Cold War escalated, then suddenly ended. As the Star Wars missile system and railway cars carrying mobile nuclear missile launchers were discussed, the military revamped its methods and technology. Smart bombs, stealth aircraft, and myriad other inventions made warfare possible with little loss of American lives. Since September 11, 2001, concern about terrorism has dominated discussion of spending on weapons and the military.

Concern about pollution and the environment is less often perceived as a pro-life issue. Recent research demonstrates links between global warming, nonsustainable methods of agriculture and industry, and threats to the health and well-being of individuals and regions. Americans express concern about the environment, but few rank it as a top priority.

Each of these issues has been studied in depth within a constellation of related questions. Euthanasia and abortion are often debated within a framework of human autonomy; care for the poor and welfare in contrast to responsibility and employment. Capital punishment is caught up in a swirl of issues: an inadequate criminal justice system, victims' rights, and changing community standards. Only a few question the morality of military technologies, even those that clearly target or impact civilian lives. Military spending is criticized by those who call for reduced taxes; respect-for-life is rarely part of the conversation. Environmental concerns, too, are framed in an instrumental context: what will make the economy grow and support the high-consumption American lifestyle? Voices that ask whether this way of life is good for humans, or sustainable for humanity, are marginalized.

The thread of respect for life, woven among these issues, is not often visible in the public forum, where political ideologies dominate the analysis. Traditional liberals favor government intervention to "support life" by improving the opportunities available to the poorest members of society, but oppose legal limits on issues deemed to be matters of private morality. Traditional conservatives attempt to reduce government intervention in the economy, but promote legal restraints to protect vulnerable human life. Each perspective both shares and disputes some of the policy mandates that flow from the consistent ethic of life.[2]

The consistent ethic is particularly interesting for the breadth and diversity of issues it weaves together, drawn from both sides of deep and long-standing ideological divides. Cardinal Bernardin drew together questions of individual and social morality in a unique way, one that would make common cause with both liberals and conservatives, although that was not his goal.[3]

More surprising was the rapid dissemination of the notion of a "seamless garment." The phrase was apt and easy to understand, capturing the imagination. In the early 1980s, though, American culture was perceived as secularized; religion was becoming a private matter whose influence over major decisions, both public and private, was weak or nonexistent.[4] Shortly after the concept of the seamless garment came into popular parlance, one sociologist (J. Stephen Cleghorn) termed Bernardin's role that of a prophet standing against the tide of secularization.[5] Robert Wuthnow, in his sweeping review of American spirituality at the end of the twentieth century, described a revolution in the nature of moral and religious thinking. Americans had moved away from freedom of religion—the freedom to live according to the teachings and practices of particular denominations—to consider religious freedom in terms of freedom of choice.[6] That term, often associated with the abortion debate, is perhaps the ethical opposite of the seamless garment proposition. Wuthnow found that the individualistic trend in American culture and spirituality decouples moral issues one from another, and stands against the imposition of any external, objective framework for morality.

This chapter explores the relevance and trajectory of the consistent ethic of life in the decades leading up to the new millennium. Does the evidence indicate the concept of the seamless garment fits patterns of public opinion? In the face of the countervailing trends toward individualism and secularization, has this proposition had an impact? Data from the 1972–2004 General Social Survey (GSS) were used to answer these questions. The GSS, a highly regarded and professionally implemented survey of American public opinion, includes questions on each of these pro-life issues. The analysis demonstrates the level of support for each pro-life issue, how it has changed over time, and whether support for a *consistent ethic of life* is visible or growing among Americans.

ATTITUDES ON RESPECT-FOR-LIFE ISSUES

A brief examination of the history of support for each of the pro-life issues, and some examination of the characteristics of those who show strong support, provides a foundation for examining the extent to which they cohere into a seamless garment.

Capital Punishment

Historically, all nations of the world have used the death penalty. Western Europe, beginning with Portugal in 1867, banned capital punishment for all ordinary crimes. Even in countries where popular support for the death penalty was high, the decision to abolish it did not spark extended public debate, and abolition is now a central principle in international diplomatic and political organizations. Even in the face of horrendous genocides, neither the International Criminal Court nor the Criminal Tribunals for the former Yugoslavia and Rwanda makes provision for capital punishment. Candidates for membership in the European Union are required to abolish the death penalty prior to admission. As of 2006, 123 nations have abandoned capital punishment in their laws (97) or in practice (26), while 73 nations, primarily in the Middle East, Asia, and Africa, retain it. The United States and Japan are unique among developed nations in retaining the death penalty.

In the United States, opposition to the death penalty has not exceeded 40 percent of the population. The proportion of GSS respondents who opposed capital punishment dropped steadily through the 1990s, even as the Supreme Court decisions limited jury discretion, amplified the appeals process, and overturned its use for the mentally retarded and juvenile offenders. The discovery that several death row inmates were innocent, first in Illinois and then in other states, resulted in an upswing in opposition to the death penalty. In 2004, however, only one out of three survey respondents expressed opposition.

Throughout the 1970s and 1980s, those who had no religious affiliation were slightly more likely to oppose capital punishment than those who claimed a religious identity. During the 1990s, when overall levels of opposition were quite low, Jewish respondents and members of other religious groups also were slightly more likely to oppose capital punishment. Even with the introduction of the consistent ethic of life, and Pope John Paul II's public forgiveness of his intended assassin, Catholics did not express greater opposition to the death penalty than others. In the 1990s and early twenty-first century, Catholics, Protestants, and members of non-Christian religions who attended religious services more than once a month were more likely to oppose capital punishment, but even among these groups, fewer than half oppose capital punishment.

End-of-Life Issues

Elizabeth Kübler-Ross's *On Death and Dying* was published just as the first GSS survey was fielded and hospice care for the terminally ill was a new and novel concept. The survey results reflect public opinion as Jack Kevorkian, Oregon's legalization of physician-assisted suicide, and the battle to remove Terry Schiavo's feeding tube held the public eye. The GSS delves into two aspects of this topic: whether terminally ill patients should be allowed to die (to refuse all treatment except comfort care) and whether a terminally ill patient has a right to commit suicide. The first question corresponds approximately to support or opposition to choosing hospice care over extraordinary medical measures. The second, while it fails to consider whether a third party can assist, definitely taps into the dimension of support for individual autonomy in choosing the time and manner of death.

Survey respondents in the United States show significantly more opposition to a "right" to suicide than to allowing terminally ill patients to refuse further care, although the gap closed in the two decades from 1976 to 1996. More than half of the respondents opposed a right to suicide in 1976, but the level of opposition fell steadily until 1996. Referenda on assisted suicide in several states kindled widespread public debate, leading to a slight increase in opposition to a *right* to suicide. Protestants, Catholics, and those who follow non–Judeo-Christian religions show significantly more opposition to a right to suicide than do Jews and those with no religious affiliation—although the latter also show an increase in opposition in the years since 1996.

Abortion

No issue has received so much attention over such a long period of time—with so little evidence of change in the opinion of the general populace in the GSS Survey. Moreover, many people hold a variety of opinions on the issue, opposing legal abortion under some circumstances, supporting it in others. Barely 10 percent of Americans oppose abortion when a woman's life or health is seriously endangered—perhaps perceiving this as a choice between the loss of one life or two. On the other hand, close to 60 percent of Americans oppose making abortion legal for "any reason" that a woman might have. In general, there is significantly more opposition to abortion for "personal" or social reasons—being unmarried, married but not wanting more children, or from a low-income family—than for "external" or physical reasons such as pregnancy due to rape, probability of a serious defect in the baby, or endangerment to the mother's health or life. The gap in opposition due to these groups of factors has been relatively constant in the more than thirty years since abortion became legal across America in 1973.

Religious belief does play an important role in opposition to abortion for both personal and external reasons. Catholics and Protestants show significantly higher levels of opposition to abortion, even in the hard circumstances where there is little opposition overall. The distinction is even clearer with regard to the personal rationales. At least 60 percent of those who identify themselves as Catholics or Protestants oppose abortion "for any reason," while only about 30 percent of those with no religious affiliation and even fewer Jewish respondents express opposition.

Help for the Poor

Beyond the issues that relate to imminent death, the consistent ethic of life encompasses the ways in which society assists and protects its poorest citizens. In all the surveys from 1972 to the present, barely 20 percent agreed that the government was spending too little on welfare. Yet when, beginning in 1984, some of the respondents were asked a slightly different version of the question—that the government was spending too little to "help" or "care for" the poor—the proportion that agreed jumped to nearly 70 percent. It is impossible to determine whether this difference reflects negative stereotypes regarding welfare recipients, or endorsement of a socially desirable but vague value of helping the poor.

Spending for Military

With the end of the Cold War in 1989 and with increasing awareness of violent and genocidal regimes and terrorism, fewer Americans now view spending on armaments and the military in terms of threats to respect for life. In post–September 11 America, in fact, military spending is sometimes portrayed as support for life. The proportion of Americans who think the government is spending "too much" on the military and armaments has fluctuated greatly, reflecting our involvement with challenges and threats from abroad.

Within these fluctuations, though, a second pattern is visible, one related to differences in religion. Catholics and, until the mid-1990s, Jews were much more likely to call military spending excessive, and Protestants the least likely.

Spending for the Environment

Public opinion on the environment is, perhaps, the most surprising among these respect-for-life issues; across more than three decades, more than half of those surveyed stated the government was spending too little on "improving and protecting" the environment. This issue is particularly salient to those who do not affiliate with a religion: at least 70 percent of this group found government spending too low. Catholics and Protestants only reached that level of support for improving the environment once, during 1988–1991, indicating they are less likely to connect this issue with their religious beliefs.

PATTERNS IN PUBLIC OPINION ON RESPECT-FOR-LIFE ISSUES

This brief overview of public opinion on six important respect-for-life issues reveals a major barrier to protecting the lives and well-being of the most vulnerable members of our society; *respect for life* is rarely a dominant perspective on any of these issues. Within a democratic system, legislation to protect vulnerable life on any of these issues is unlikely to gain approval. This hard reality perhaps spurred Cardinal Bernardin's decision to assert the importance of a consistent ethic of life, uniting these issues, rather than to speak out on a small number of them. Yet, anyone who has been active in the marketplace of ideas and social action knows that different groups form the majority that opposes each of these issues. The person pressing for the death penalty for a convicted killer one day may be seen protesting assisted suicide or abortion on demand another day. Are there patterns of opinion among these issues, or do Americans develop an attitude on each, unrelated to the others?

The most direct approach is simply to count: when asked about a series of issues, how many of a person's responses correspond with the seamless garment position? When this method is applied to the nearly 27,000 GSS respondents, the results are revealing. Their support or opposition to the pro-life position was tallied in eight areas: capital punishment, the physical and the social abortion rationales, military spending, welfare spending, passive and active euthanasia, and spending for the environment. Fewer than one in ten people offer *no* opinions that support a respect-for-life position and only about six people out of 100 give six or more positive responses, corresponding to a consistent ethic of life. More than half of this large representative sample of Americans report a pro-life opinion on three, four, or five of the questions—but no more.

The results are the same in the analysis of groups representing three- or four-year time ranges: the proportion supporting no, a few, some, and most seamless garment issues is stable across time. When religion is considered, two groups—those who did not identify with any religion or were Jewish—were significantly more likely to support fewer than three seamless garment positions. The differences were small, only one or two percentage points, and the sample included relatively few members of these groups. Catholics who reported a strong affiliation with their faith were significantly more likely to show support for six or more ethic of life issues, especially in the five years immediately following Cardinal Bernadin's speech. Even among strongly religious Catholics, the people most likely to hear and be receptive to the consistent ethic of life, only 15 percent ever expressed support for all or most of the issues.

These results offer both hope and caution to proponents of a consistent ethic of life. Few Americans hold a set of opinions diametrically opposed to an ethic of life. At the same time, even fewer Americans express views that correspond consistently to positions that protect the vulnerable and support life. This suggests that Americans' opinions on these issues are influenced by other factors. Their attitudes may be shaped by the alternative positions with regard to each issue, or by other, competing, ideological or ethical positions.

Another possibility is simply that Americans do not, in general, perceive these issues as related. Many connect with the legalization of assisted suicide and abortion, but fewer recognize their relationship with abolishing the death penalty, and fewer still the association with spending for the poor, the environment, or weaponry. While respondents were not asked whether they perceive connections among these issues, it is possible to explore this possibility using factor analysis, a statistical technique that seeks underlying dimensions reflected in the observed responses to survey questions. The procedure extracts underlying factors and shows how strongly each survey question is related to, or "loads," on each factor. If all the questions are strongly related, as the consistent ethic would predict, a single factor will be extracted.

The results of this analysis for all time periods from 1974 to the present indicate a division between respect-for-life issues in the domains of private morality and personal behavior (passive euthanasia, suicide, physical and social reasons for abortion) and those that involve social policies (capital punishment, military spending, welfare spending, and environmental spending). This supports Cleghorn's contention—based on research at the time of the Seamless Garment speech—that people tend to divide the issues into private and public spheres.[7]

The results for attitudes on capital punishment, however, suggest that a more consistent ethic may be developing. In the 1970s and 1980s, this issue loaded only with the public sphere. Beginning in the mid-1990s, Americans' attitudes regarding the death penalty were somewhat related to both dimensions. This was even more pronounced among Catholics with a strong affiliation to their faith. Members of this group were more likely to respond similarly to the death penalty and to "personal" issues such as abortion and euthanasia.

The GSS provides evidence, however, that there has also been erosion from a consistent ethic of life among those who *do* hold respect-for-life positions on the policy issues. Throughout the 1990s, the factor that includes a positive view on welfare and environmental spending and a negative view on military spending *also* includes a weak loading in support of voluntary suicide. The debates about assisted suicide, from the time of Dr. Jack Kevorkian's first foray into the field through the legalization of assisted suicide in Oregon to the present, often use the rhetoric of "quality of life." This might persuade people who are already concerned about the quality of life—for the poor, those affected by our military engagements, and polluted environments—to support another position on "the quality of life."

Political ideologies provide a promising potential explanation for the pattern of attitudes observed among Americans. The personal morality at the core of the Personal Life Ethic factor is strongly associated with conservatism, while concern for increased spending for welfare and the environment, decreased military spending, and opposition to the death penalty—the Policy Life Ethic factor—are traditionally liberal positions. Scores for the Personal Life Ethic and the Policy Life Ethic show weak, but significant, correlations with political ideology. Those who support a pro-life position on the private morality issues are more likely to call themselves conservative, while those who endorse a pro-life position on the policy issues are more likely to consider themselves liberal. These correlations are so weak, however, that they do not make a convincing argument that political ideology can explain Americans' attitudes on these questions.

Other analyses show that education also has a complex impact on respect-for-life attitudes. People who have higher levels of education express support for fewer of the Personal Life Ethic positions and more of the Policy Life Ethic positions than people with less education. Similarly, identification with the Democratic Party is associated with less opposition to euthanasia and abortion, more support for spending on welfare and environment and less on the military, and the abolition of capital punishment.

UNDERSTANDING PUBLIC OPINION

These results certainly present a complex picture, one that defies any simplistic interpretation. If anything, they give ample evidence that the salience of these issues has failed to produce acceptance of any single ideological approach. The consistent ethic of life is one among many in the marketplace of ideas in modern America.

There are, however, some conclusions to draw and hints of further avenues for research and social activism. The most obvious is the fact that most Americans show, at best, moderate support for a range of seamless garment positions. Nonetheless, the evidence of small increases in the number of people who support pro-life positions in the first years of the twenty-first century cannot be overlooked. Moreover, those who hold the strongest pro-life position on abortion are increasingly expressing opposition to capital punishment.[8] Recent history shows that life issues are being recognized as politically important and salient. For many, pro-life positions on abortion are among their most important criteria in casting their votes. Assisted suicide initiatives have been defeated in many states. Concern with the equity, and even the accuracy, of the administration of capital punishment led many governors to delay or halt executions. Clearly, issues central to the consistent ethic carry significant weight in the political arena. Why, then, does public opinion seem to show otherwise? Why is the seamless garment such a poor fit?

Questions added to the GSS in 1991 and 1998 provide a clue. In those years, the survey asked if abortion was *wrong* if serious defects in the baby were suspected—as well as asking whether abortion should be legally available. Surprisingly, more than half of the people who stated that such abortions would always or almost always be wrong nonetheless supported the proposition that abortion should be legal. This supports Wuthnow's contention that American individualism has decoupled morality from religion, with most ethical decisions seen as within the purview of each person. Similar freedom-of-choice arguments have been made about assisted suicide.

The consistent ethic of life makes a fundamentally different claim. In fact, the seamless garment ethic questions whether we, in our personal autonomy, have a right to make these choices on an individualistic basis. The findings from the GSS suggest that many who accept the behavioral implications of opposition to abortion for themselves either do not grasp or do not agree with the foundational principle that deeming an action "wrong" should have an impact in the policy arena as well as one's personal life. This combination of individualism and relativism undermines the pursuit of social policies on the basis of morality.

TAILORING THE SEAMLESS GARMENT

When he proposed the consistent ethic of life, Cardinal Bernardin was stating a vision, not reporting on how Americans currently viewed these issues. "I am convinced," he said, "that the pro-life position of the Church must be *developed* in terms of a comprehensive and consistent ethic of life" and affirmed that he was "committed to *shaping* a position of linkage among the life issues." When Bernardin first used the image of the seamless garment, late in 1983, he expanded thinking on the two life issues that were most prominent at the time, nuclear war and abortion, to include the death penalty, euthanasia, poverty and welfare reform, health care, racism, and pornography. The theological foundation for these issues was, he said, the "*defense* of the person."[9] In the two decades since, the logic of his argument and its moral implications were widely disseminated, shaping much of the dialogue surrounding these issues. What opportunities exist for those who continue to weave the seamless garment today?

The logic of the consistent ethic of life is, perhaps, most clear in situations where the life of a single individual is held in sway: abortion, euthanasia, and capital punishment. It can be argued that the lives in question are qualitatively different: the unborn life is certainly innocent, that of the death row inmate presumably is not, and assisted suicide presumes that the terminally ill person herself no longer wishes to live. Nonetheless, the foundational goal of the *defense of the person* is most easily seen and least likely to be debated. These are also the issues in which there has been some increase, however small, in support for positions that respect life. This grouping—drawing together issues from both sides of the liberal-conservative divide—may be an effective arena in which to promote the consistent ethic of life. The data from public opinion surveys hint that people who already hold a pro-life position on one of these issues may be more likely to adopt such a position on the others.

The ethic of life is explicitly applied to government spending on welfare, health care, and the environment less often than to the high-profile issues of abortion and the death penalty. While people who hold a progressive political ideology often link these issues and hold similar positions on all of them, the linkage to life-and-death choices is not always apparent. For instance, increased welfare spending may have contributed to some of the decrease in the number of abortions performed in the latter part of the 1990s. Poor women have the greatest freedom of choice when faced with an unexpected pregnancy if there are adequate financial and social support systems that allow them to choose to continue the pregnancy and raise the child. The divide between conservative and progressive positions often pits "autonomy" against "morality" where the consistent ethic of life might open new perspectives and opportunities.

Legal scholar Thomas Berg outlines the existing ideological frameworks shaping American politics and social policy. The solid conservatives take pro-life positions on abortion and euthanasia but have a different view on welfare, the environment, and war. On the other hand, solid liberals support initiatives to improve welfare and the environment and abolish capital punishment but do not recognize any connection with pro-life positions on abortion or euthanasia. Berg points out that even those who are liberal on personal issues but conservative when it comes to economic, social, and foreign policy have a recognized position—"laissez-faire"—and a political party—the Libertarians.

The fourth alternative—conservative on cultural and moral issues but liberal on matters of economic and foreign policy—has not been recognized as either an ideological or political position. Berg demonstrates that some social activists—as pro-life feminists, liberal evangelicals, and Catholic social justice groups—promote a "pro-life progressivism" that embodies the consistent ethic of life.[10] The existing political taxonomy, which shapes the discourse and even the thought processes of many Americans, does not recognize or make room for this position. The fact that the GSS finds, even over a thirty-year period, so few people who hold this configuration of positions is therefore not surprising.

A summary statement of the American public opinion on pro-life progressivism is short and simple. Few Americans hold attitudes consistent with the seamless garment. Yet this apparently bleak picture does not tell the entire story. The slight shifts seen in public opinion are echoes of the ongoing change in death penalty practice, abortion rates, and economic and ecological policies related to globalization and oil prices. For American public opinion to find a better fit with the seamless garment will require the work of many tailors, shaping disparate ideas around the common priority of defense of all persons, especially those who are the most vulnerable.

NOTES AND REFERENCES

1. Elam-Evans, L., Strauss, L., Herndon, J., Parker, W., Bowens, S., Zane, S., Berg, C.J. 2003. *Abortion Surveillance—United States, 2000*. Atlanta, GA: Center for Disease Control and Prevention.

2. Sawyer, Darwin O. 1982. Public Attitudes Toward Life and Death. *Public Opinion Quarterly, 46*, 521–533.

3. Berg, T. C. 2005. Pro-life Progressivism and the Fourth Option in American Public Life. *University of St. Thomas Law Journal, 2*(2), 235–245.

4. Chaves, M. 1994. Secularization as Declining Religious Authority. *Social Forces, 72*, 749–774.

5. Cleghorn, J. S. 1986. Respect for Life: Research Notes on Cardinal Bernardin's "Seamless Garment." *Review of Religious Research, 28*, 129–142.

6. Wuthnow, R. 1998. *After Heaven: Spirituality in America Since the 1950s*. Berkeley: University of California Press.

7. Cleghorn, Respect for Life.

8. Kelly, James R., & Kudlac, C. April 1, 2000. Pro-life, Anti-Death Penalty. *America, 182*(11), 6–8. See also Chapter 16 in this book.

9. Fuechtmann, T. G. (ed.). 1987. *Consistent Ethic of Life: Joseph Cardinal Bernardin.* Kansas City, MO: Sheed & Ward.

10. Berg, Pro-life Progressivism and the Fourth Option in American Public Life.

Perceptions of Connections

Rachel M. MacNair

The following is a report on two of the studies that have been conducted by the research arm of Consistent Life, the Institute for Integrated Social Analysis. Rachel M. MacNair, PhD, is its Director and conducted the studies.

WHAT SCHOLARS HAVE STUDIED

Scholarly literature considering connecting issues is rather sparse. The longest look taken on the issue is by Kimberly Cook, in a 1998 book with in-depth interviews of thirty people on abortion and the death penalty.[1] She divided people into four groups: favoring both, opposing both, and each way of favoring one and opposing the other. She labeled them with their abortion position first and death penalty second: choice/life, choice/death, life/life, and life/death. Cook was choice/life.

She asked the interviewees whether they saw a connection between the two issues. The choice/life group showed a concern for the socially disadvantaged, an anticontrol attitude and disdain for punitiveness, and a concern for personal autonomy, along with the belief that the flawed legal system should not interfere with life and death decisions. The choice/death group did not see the issues as connected but offered the suggestion that people be held accountable—for a child or a crime. The life/life group emphasized compassion and had less disdain for the government, with a value-of-life ethic that all killing is wrong and illogical, and violence as a solution causes more violence.

The life/death group saw the best protection of innocent human life as important, requiring a serious penalty for those who take it.

In 1991, Clagget and Schafer made the same divisions.[2] But they named the groups differently with a different logic. Those who supported both abortion and capital punishment were called "pro-choice," believing that the collectivity can adopt policies for taking life when needed. Those opposing both were called "pro-life," consistently rejecting any right to take lives. Those supporting capital punishment while opposing abortion were "just deserts," supporting taking the life of the guilty but not the innocent. And those opposing capital punishment and supporting abortion were "original sin," rejecting taking a developed life but not believing that the undeveloped has any moral claim to living.

They obtained data from a 1987 American public opinion survey. African-Americans had the largest share in the "pro-life" cell and had the closest balance among the four types. The only two groups with a majority in any single group were "born-again" Protestants, with 54 percent supporting capital punishment but opposing abortion, and the non-Christians, with 55 percent supporting both. Within the "pro-life" and "pro-choice" cells, the percentages of Democrats and Republicans were nearly identical.

Lester, Hadley, and Lucas tested students on personality differences by offering questionnaires that measured different personality characteristics. They found small personality differences on war and euthanasia, but none on capital punishment or abortion.[3]

Johnson and Tamney studied the capital punishment positions of abortion opponents. They divided the participants into the "inconsistent," who opposed abortion but favored the death penalty, and the "consistent," who opposed both. They found the inconsistent to be more traditional and more concerned with sexual morality.[4]

Some studies did factor analyses on life-and-death issue positions, and uniformly had a two-factor solution. Abortion and euthanasia (with assisted suicide, other forms of suicide, and refusal of treatment) go in one factor, and capital punishment with military positions (war, arms buildup, military spending) in the other. This division was also found in the national opinion data,[5] in two student samples,[6] and even in data as far back as 1963.[7]

Researchers vary widely in interpretations of data. Kalish proposes a liberal/conservative dichotomy. Beswick suggests the categories "proactive killing," taking human life for social engineering in abortion and euthanasia, and "reactive killing," self-protective in war and executions. Lester, Hadley, and Lucas thought that death is of two types, of either one's self or the other. Death of self applies in abortion because of the identification of parent with fetus. Cleghorn suggested the *personal* nature of abortion and euthanasia and *political* nature of war and the death penalty.

TWO LARGE STUDIES

Study 1 focuses on abortion and capital punishment, with both open-ended questions and statements where people rated on a scale of 1–5 how much they agreed or disagreed with them. These were designed to consider points raised by earlier scholars, testing with a far larger group. Study 2 expanded to include war and euthanasia, with almost entirely open-ended questions.

Study 1 used a paper-and-pencil questionnaire. People were asked their position on abortion and the death penalty, and then whether the two were connected. Open-ended questions asked what the connections and differences were. There were 103 from an insert in an urban, politics-oriented newspaper, 40 from libraries, 18 from political events, 150 from classes in an inner-city junior college, and 153 direct personal solicitations at coffee shops—a total of 464.

Study 2 was an online survey. People were asked their positions on five issues: abortion, military spending, the death penalty, the use of force, and assisted suicide. People were then asked if they saw any connections between each of the six possible combinations of the four issues of abortion, death penalty, euthanasia, and war. In text boxes they could give short answers to what the connections were.

We sent notice to several electronic listservs, the ones primarily dealing with one of the issues. This deliberately gets responses from opinionated people. The completed surveys totaled 699.

The positions were the same in both studies. Because many object to a strict dichotomy, three positions were offered for each, two extremes and a middle. There were still complaints of inadequate nuance. For abortion: pro-choice, middle ground, and pro-life. For the death penalty: "It should be done more often," "It should be done only with strict due process," or "I oppose it in all cases." In Study 2, for spending on arms, the options were "My country should spend more," "My country should spend the same," or "My country should spend less than it does now." For the use of force, the options were, "My country should use it more than it does now," "It should be used with caution," or "It should not be used, with rare if any exceptions." Positions were worded this way because previous experience showed that simply asking people their position on "war" is unfunctional; almost everyone is against it unless it is necessary. For assisted suicide, the options were, "I believe in an individual's right to die," "It should be allowed, but only with rigid safeguards," or "I oppose it in all cases." On each issue, the first two options categorized the person as favoring and the third as opposing when placing into four groupings. For other purposes, the difference between the first and second option indicated strength of feeling.

Questions: Both Studies

The question of perceiving connectedness between the issues was determined by taking into account the percentages of people answering "yes" to the question "Do you see these issues as connected?"

The second question was what the major connections and differences were. This was asked in an open-ended way rather than in the form of a checklist, to find out what people bring up on their own.

In both the studies, people were asked to rate themselves on a conservative/liberal continuum.

Questions: Study 1 Only

Kimberly Cook thought that punitiveness and intolerance would be highest in those opposing abortion and favoring the death penalty. With the pro-death penalty position, abortion opposition would not be based on a principle of valuing human life but on a desire to punish sexually misbehaving women by forcing them into childbirth. She did not cite any right-to-life literature for the concept of childbirth being more punishing than abortion itself; such an idea would startle most pro-life people. However, these studies included nonactivists, and the first study included a test of this thesis.

With no established scales to test punitiveness or intolerance, I wrote items to measure them. The item "Even the vilest criminal remains a human being" came from Supreme Court Justice William Brennan.[8] Supreme Court Justice Thurgood Marshall wrote, "[T]he finality of a capital sentence obliges society to ensure that defendants get a fair chance to present all available defenses."[9] Both these men asserted these as principles on which all reasonable people agree. Three more items came from a previous survey: "Society has the right to get revenge when a murder has been committed," "There are some murderers whose death would give me satisfaction," and "Any execution would make me sad, regardless of the crime committed."[10]

Cook also thought the groups differed on solutions. A section of the survey offered solutions according to her suggestions, which people rated as "crucial," "a good idea," "no effect," "a bad idea," "or strongly oppose." This would also be a test of punitiveness.

Questions: Study 2 Only

Since Study 2 expanded to a greater number of issues, we can explore previous findings on a two-factor model. Do more people answer "yes" to whether the issues of abortion and euthanasia are connected, and to whether the issues of war and the death penalty are connected, than to the other issue combinations?

RESULTS

For Study 1, there were 247 women and 203 men, in the age range of 14 to 82, the average age being 34.4 years. There were 334 Whites, 46 Blacks, 18 Hispanics, 9 Asian, 5 of other ethnicities, and 27 refused to disclose their ethnicities. In the position groupings, 8.6 percent opposed both abortion and the death penalty, 53.2 percent favored both, 18.3 percent favored abortion and opposed the death penalty, and 19.8 percent opposed abortion and favored the death penalty.

For Study 2, the sample of 699 subjects had 426 women and 254 men, in the age range of 13 to 81, the average age being 36.6 years. The racial makeup of this group was almost entirely White. Position groupings were as follows: 19.2 percent opposing both abortion and the death penalty, 31.0 percent favoring both, 41.2 percent favoring abortion and opposing the death penalty, and 8.6 percent opposing abortion but favoring the death penalty.

The abortion/death penalty positions were the only ones asked for in the first study, but they are also handy designations in the second study. People are clearer about their positions on those two issues. Many indicated that they had not thought about euthanasia much. Previous experience shows that most people will oppose war unless it is necessary, a continuum of opinions rather than group divisions.

When the two studies asked something the same way, the results could be combined. The sample size would then be 1,163 people.

Questions from Both Studies: Are the Issues Connected?

Findings confirmed previous research. In both studies, over 80 percent of those who oppose both answered "yes." Those who favor both were lowest in the percentage answering "yes." Each of the two groups who favor one and

Table 11.1. Percentage of Those Answering Yes

Group	1	2	3	4
Abortion/death penalty, Study 1	81.1%	37.8%	57.5%	43.8%
Abortion/death penalty, Study 2	88.1%	26.0%	40.7%	36.8%
Abortion/euthanasia	93.2%	49.2%	*	*
Euthanasia/war	71.1%	20.7%	26.3%	24.6%
War/death penalty	80.0%	30.1%	62.1%	45.6%
Euthanasia/death penalty	80.2%	24.2%	52.9%	29.8%
Abortion/war	78.3%	17.5%	19.5%	39.4%

Group 1: oppose both; Group 2: favor both (war measured by "use of force" position); Group 3: favor first issue listed, oppose second; Group 4: oppose first issue, favor second.

*Groups 3 and 4 were too small to generate usable percentages.

oppose the other are in between (see Table 11.1). This pattern was also seen across the different issues in the second study.

Furthermore, those with the extreme position in favor saw less connection than those who selected the middle ground position (see Table 11.2). The pattern is very strong except for assisted suicide.

Table 11.2. Percentage of Those Answering Yes, Issues Are Connected, by Level of Position

Position	1	2	3
Abortion/euthanasia			
Abortion position	48.6%	51.5%	80.0%
Assisted suicide	50.8%	46.3%	87.7%
Euthanasia/war			
Assisted suicide	24.5%	25.8%	59.9%
Use of force	17.2%	26.2%	41.6%
War/death penalty			
Use of force	21.4%	65.7%	72.5%
Death penalty	28.4%	35.8%	72.8%
Death penalty/abortion			
Death penalty	19.4%	31.2%	55.3%
Abortion	28.5%	51.1%	72.3%
Euthanasia/death penalty			
Assisted suicide	27.4%	34.2%	67.5%
Death penalty	22.6%	25.8%	47.9%
Abortion/war			
Abortion	18.6%	39.1%	68.9%
Use of force	17.9%	29.9%	44.4%

Position 1: definitely favor; Position 2: middle ground; Position 3: definitely oppose.

Table 11.3. Major Connections and Differences, Abortion and Death Penalty (1,163 People)

Group	−ab/−dp	+ab/+dp	+ab/−dp	−ab/+dp
Connection: Causing Death				
Study 1	87.9%	9.2%	69.4%	80.0%
Study 2	94.6%	67.9%	82.4%	90.0%
Connection: Choice/Government Should Not Interfere				
Study 1	0	2.2%	17.6%	0
Study 2	0	0	3.5%	0
Difference: Innocence vs. Guilt				
Study 1	57.9%	35.1%	10.9%	77.6%
Study 2	70.4%	29.1%	17.6%	76.4%
Difference: Fetus Not Fully Formed				
Study 1	.002%	14.9%	26.1%	.002%
Study 2	0	16.5%	42.0%	0
Difference: Personal/Political				
Study 1	.002%	8.1%	15.2%	0
Study 2	8.3%	9.7%	8.3%	0

\+ = favor; − = oppose; ab = abortion; dp = death penalty.

Questions from Both Studies: How Are Abortion and the Death Penalty Connected, and How Do They Differ?

Table 11.3 shows the major connections and differences. Variations on causing death—termination of a life, sacredness of life, killing—were by far the most common mentioned, with at least two-thirds of the comments mentioning this in all groups. A previous study showed that even among 130 abortion doctors and nurses, 77 percent brought up the theme of abortion as a destructive act, as destroying a living thing.[11]

One of the two biggest differences involved the innocent/guilty distinction. Abortion opponents who favor the death penalty find this a major concern, with those who oppose both being next highest. Among those who favor abortion availability, those who favor the death penalty are more likely to bring this up than those who oppose it.

Questions from Both Studies: Conservative/Liberal

The conservative/liberal continuum had scores from 1 to 6, ranging from ultraconservative to radical, and an option of "other." Taking only the scores of those who placed themselves on the conservative/liberal continuum, the scores were as Cook predicted for her choice/life (liberal, average 4.49) and

Table 11.4. Liberal/Conservative Self-Designation

Group	−ab/−dp	+ab/+dp	+ab/−dp	−ab/+dp
Mean Score on Continuum	3.74	3.48	4.49	2.55
Distribution				
1 ultra-conservative	1.2%	2.6%	0.3%	7.0%
2 conservative	10.6%	8.1%	1.1%	29.2%
3 moderate	27.1%	32.6%	12.5%	31.0%
4 liberal	19.4%	34.5%	33.3%	10.5%
5 ultra-liberal	1.8%	3.1%	13.6%	.002%
6 radical	15.3%	4.7%	21.4%	.002%
"Other"	24.7%	14.1%	17.9%	10.5%

+ = favor; − = oppose; ab = abortion; dp = death penalty.

life/death groups (conservative, average 2.55). However, Cook was incorrect in predicting the other two groups. The choice/death was more conservative (3.48), the life/life more liberal (3.74).

An interesting pattern emerges with those who answered "other." Overall, 16.5 percent thereby refused to go on a conservative/liberal continuum. The two abortion-supporting groups were close to this overall percentage (17.9 percent of death penalty opponents and 14.1 percent of proponents). However, there was a clear difference between the two pro-life groups. Only 10.5 percent of those favoring the death penalty answered "other," but almost a quarter, 24.7 percent, of those opposing the death penalty did so.

Note in Table 11.4 that the pro-life group opposing capital punishment was more spread out, along with having only three-quarters willing to be on the spectrum at all. This group is more likely, then, to have people who identify themselves as conservative but oppose the death penalty or who identify themselves as liberal or radical but oppose abortion.

Questions from Study 1 Only

I did a factor analysis to see if the items to which people answered agree/disagree would coalesce together, but it failed. There is no statistical justification for using a set of items together to make a score for the ideas of punitiveness, revenge, or intolerance. Taking items that measured punitiveness individually, no groups varied substantially (see Table 11.5). Those favoring capital punishment affirmed a vengeful attitude more than its opponents, as would be expected, but no large difference emerged between proponents of the death penalty based on their abortion positions. If there were such a group,

Table 11.5. Study 1: Answers on Selected Likert Items (1 = agree / 5 = disagree)

Group	−ab/−dp	+ab/+dp	+ab/−dp	−ab/+dp
Even the vilest criminal remains a human being	1.24	2.79	1.54	2.33
There are some murderers whose death would give me satisfaction	4.32	2.48	4.00	2.72
Any execution would make me sad, regardless of the crime committed	1.84	3.49	2.00	3.01
Women who've had abortions are often troubled by them	1.47	2.20	2.00	1.54
Those troubled by their abortions deserve emotional support and help	1.64	1.73	1.39	1.72
Women who've had abortions are all going to hell	4.11	4.73	4.78	4.21
Giving birth rather than aborting a child you can't handle is immoral	4.46	3.26	3.47	4.35
A major problem with abortion is that it encourages sexual promiscuity	2.59	3.53	3.77	1.92
My entire family agrees with me on the death penalty	3.51	3.01	3.15	2.74
My entire family agrees with me on abortion	2.89	3.16	3.05	2.56
I trust the police	3.11	3.33	3.31	2.84
Women should be welcome and equal in the paid work force	1.25	1.21	1.16	1.43
Those who disagree with me on abortion are evil	4.11	4.52	4.54	4.17
Those who disagree with me on the death penalty are evil	4.24	4.56	4.50	4.27

+ = favor; − = oppose; ab = abortion; dp = death penalty.

it was the pro-life group that was more likely to be sad at any execution and less likely to have an execution give them satisfaction.

All groups showed high agreement with the items "Women troubled by their abortions deserve emotional support and help," "Using violence to oppose abortion is never justified," "Men and women should have equality of opportunity," and "Women should be welcome in and treated equally in the paid workforce." Cook predicted that the life/death group would be most opposed to women being treated equally in the paid workforce. They did have the highest scores, indicating most disagreement, but the average was still under 1.5, where 2 indicated agreement and 1 strong agreement.

Cook predicted that the choice/death group was most likely to agree that it is irresponsible to give birth to a child one cannot handle, and this did happen. However, the difference from the choice/life group was not great, and the average showed slightly on the side of disagreement.

Johnson and Tamney predicted that the life/death group would be the most concerned about abortion encouraging sexual promiscuity. The eighth item in Table 11.5 confirms this.

Most remaining patterns simply show that people who are opposed to either abortion or the death penalty answer one way and the people in favor answer the other, without reference to their position on the other issue.

Cook predicted that the choice/life group would have the greatest mistrust of police, with a philosophy wary of legal system flaws. However, the item which simply stated "I trust the police" did not show a difference. All four groups were around the middle score of three.

On solutions for reducing abortions, most differences were, as expected, between those who do and do not favor the availability of abortion. On an item about having volunteers providing more services for pregnant women, all four groups had mean scores showing they favored this. Cook's predictions were confirmed on government services, with her life/death group following its conservative proclivities against government spending. On actually cutting welfare payments to pregnant women, the two groups opposing the death penalty had a mean score indicating opposition to it, whereas both groups favoring the death penalty were more likely to favor it; no group did so strongly. As for doing the opposite, raising welfare payments, only the life/life group had a mean tending to favor this idea.

A space for people to write additional solutions was analyzed for punitive content. Little was found, though one person suggested caning criminals, one suggested castration of sex offenders, and one said that executions should be public and humiliating. These were in the choice/death group. However, to the question on the difference between the two issues, three people in the choice/life group said the death penalty actually let people off the hook too easily, that life imprisonment would be more and better punishment.

The desire to know the results of the survey paralleled the pattern of belief about connections. Most of those requesting the results were in the life/life group (49 percent); the choice/life and life/death groups had 34 percent and 39 percent of them, respectively and only 27 percent were from the choice/death group.

Table 11.6. Study 2: Connections

A/E	E/W	W/D	D/A	D/E	A/W	
232	**161**	**268**	**215**	**164**	**142**	Variants of Causing Death
	3	46	3	6	3	Both are approved, done, or decided by State or govt.
1		41		1		Both kill enemy, wrongdoers, guilty; punish
115	7		1	2	1	Choice, autonomy, individual rights, control of body
42	2		3	4	1	Quality of life, prevent or end suffering
7	8	24	7	8	12	Done by powerful, or against powerless
		11		4		Both protect, defend
2	4	3		2	6	Done for greed, economic gain
1	7	1			2	Nazi historical connection
5	6	15	6	9	9	Similar motivation, philosophical foundation
6	15	40	12	8	12	Both solve problems with violence—disapprove
5	10	3	10	13	8	Both solve problems for perps, not victims—disapprove
6	3	7	8	8		Both solve problems—approve
4	3	7	2	2	6	Both solve problems, no approval or disapproval clear
				10		Similar or analogous procedures
12						Medical component, professional help
4	3	13	9	7	6	One is version of other

A/E = abortion/euthanasia; E/W = euthanasia/war; W/D = war/death penalty; D/A = death penalty/abortion; D/E = death penalty/euthanasia; A/W = abortion/war.

Questions from Study 2 Only: Connections and Differences

The open-ended question on connections between the issues showed variants on both causing death brought by far the largest number (see Table 11.6). Another category with many comments was their connection with choice, autonomy, individual rights, control of body, or quality of life. There were 115 comments on this connection in the abortion/euthanasia combination but very few in the other combinations.

What made the issues different? The biggest differences concerned killing the innocent versus killing the guilty in the issue combinations involving the death penalty (especially with abortion) and voluntary versus forced in all combinations involving euthanasia. That one is punishment and the other isn't was prominent in all combinations with the death penalty. Commonly mentioned under war was that it is indiscriminate or aimed at groups rather than being selective or aimed at individuals, and differences in the scale of how many people are impacted at once. That a fetus is not fully formed, sentient, conscious, alive, or is only potential was common in all the combinations with abortion.

Lester, Hadley, and Lucas suggested the death of self versus the death of other—both abortion and euthanasia aimed at self if fetus was viewed as part of self. The data did not support this, as seen in the second row of Table 11.7. The death of self rather than of someone else was a common difference between euthanasia and other issues but not once with abortion. In fact, it was listed much more frequently as a difference between euthanasia and abortion.

The difference suggested by Cleghorn—personal and political, private and public, and individual and social—arose frequently. Its frequency was especially high in contrasting either abortion or euthanasia with war, but it was also high with the death penalty. It was not mentioned as often as innocence or voluntariness, but it was a major category.

Other categories can be interpreted with the public/private theme. Choice, autonomy, and control of one's body are variants of privacy or personal theme. Being done by the State, asking someone else to kill someone else, or the identification of the target as an enemy could likewise be public or political. This does seem to be a major distinction in people's minds.

That the fetus is not fully formed and unworthy of protection was mentioned by seventy-two abortion supporters. Another eighteen saw abortion as a choice with no reference to the fetus at all. Clagget and Schafer suggested this as the logic behind the choice/life position. It is prominent, but still is only a portion of the result.

Comments which were *not* made can also be interesting. That euthanasia is not legal in most places only came up in two comments. Also, despite the difference between war and other practices being that war is more indiscriminate and aimed at groups while the others are selective and aimed at individuals, no one mentioned the selective or individual as a connection between any of the other issues.

Questions from Study 2 Only: The Two-Factor Model

The two-factor model was confirmed, because the combinations of abortion/euthanasia (56.9 percent) and war/death penalty (56.1 percent) were the only ones with the majority answering "yes" on their being connected to

Table 11.7. Study 2: Differences

A/E	E/W	W/D	D/A	D/E	A/W	
4	2	73	129	39	3	One kills innocent, other kills guilty (or accountable)
47	12			10		Death of self vs. death of other
72		2	72		24	Fetus not sentient, fully formed, conscious, alive
16			6		4	Fetus has whole life ahead, other has had some life
	3	4	3	3	3	One can fight back, other cannot
6	4			5		One victim healthy, other not
37	1	1	2		2	Age or size, beginning or end
	9	3		1	4	Intent to kill in one, merely outcome in other
1	64	26	25	30	46	Personal/political, public/private, individual/social
138	113	12	17	117	14	Voluntary versus forced
		20	38	16		One is punishment, other not
				36		One is punishment, other end to suffering
2	20		3	4	1	One prevents suffering, other causes it
3	1		18	8	4	One is choice, one is killing
5			1		1	Choice on own body vs. choice on another
	4		2	5	3	One done with malice or hate or aggression
7	26	22	14	14	12	Different justification or reasoning
	7	5	4	2	5	One can be defense or protection, other not
	20	42	2	1	9	One is selective, other is indiscriminant
1	10	33	1		7	Difference in scale, numbers killed
	10	24		2	8	Mass killing vs. one at a time/target group vs. individual
14	14	11	9	7	18	Different circumstances
5	2	3		1		Practices or tools differ
5		9	7	5		Targets differ
9	1	3	4	2	2	Different decision makers
1	4	4			1	War involves breakdown, other is orderly
13	13			3		One is peaceful or merciful, other violent or merciless
	6	3			1	One has certainty of outcome, other not
4	5	1	1	4	1	Different beneficiaries
		7	7	2		Death penalty has due process, unlike other
			3			Different politically, liberal vs. conservative
22	20	22	14	9	20	Statement of no differences seen

A/E = abortion/euthanasia; E/W = euthanasia/war; W/D = war/death penalty; D/A = death penalty/abortion; D/E = death penalty/euthanasia; A/W = abortion/war.

each other. The next highest was the death penalty and abortion, with 43.6 percent answering "yes" (comparable to Study 1, which had 46.1 percent).

The percentages for all the other combinations were much lower: 32.0 percent for euthanasia and war, 36.6 percent for euthanasia and the death penalty, and 34.2 percent for abortion and war. Yet 18.9 percent answered "yes" on all the six issue combinations, which is a slight majority on those three pairings.

Out of those who answered "yes" on only one issue combination and "no" on the rest, fifty-seven did so on abortion and euthanasia, and forty-five did so on war and the death penalty. Less than ten did so on each of the other possible issue combinations, strengthening the case that it is in these two groupings that people most see connections.

CONCLUSION

The survey results were not designed to be generalizable. In Study 1, many said they found these difficult because they had to think about things they had not thought about before. That means a proper stratified random sample poll may have trouble.

However, when people did think in terms of connections, those involving life-taking and violence emerged strongly. Would they have emerged had abortion been connected to women's issues such as equal pay and domestic violence—or to same-sex marriage and "family issues"? Would they have emerged if the death penalty were connected to crime issues, or euthanasia to medical treatment issues, or war to international relations, or if *any* of the issues were presented with entirely religious issues?

Asking about connections in an open-ended way on this specific set of issues seems to elicit the aspect of killing.

Those who see connections are most likely to be opposed to one form of violence and even more likely to be opposed to more than one, or to mark the option indicating that they are more strongly opposed. This offers reason to think that this approach of connections is useful even for those whose main concern is with any one issue.

NOTES AND REFERENCES

1. Cook, Kimberly J. 1998. *Divided Passions: Public Opinions on Abortion and the Death Penalty*. Boston: Northeastern University Press; see also Cook, K. J. (1998). A Passion to Punish: Abortion Opponents Who Favor the Death Penalty. *Justice Quarterly*, *15*, 329–356.

2. Clagget, W. J. M. and Shafer, B. E. 1991. Life and Death as Public Policy: Capital Punishment and Abortion in American Public Opinion. *International Journal of Public Opinion Research, 3,* 32–52.

3. Lester, David, Hadley, Richard A., and Lucas, William A. 1990. Personality and a Pro-death Attitude. *Personality and Individual Differences, 11,* 1183–1185.

4. Johnson, S. D. and Tamney, J. B. 1988. Factors Related to Inconsistent Life-Views. *Review of Religious Research, 30,* 40–46.

5. Cleghorn, J. S. 1986. Respect for Life: Research Notes on Cardinal Bernardin's "Seamless Garment." *Review of Religious Research, 28,* 129–142.

6. Beswick, David G. 1970. Attitudes to Taking Human Life. *Australian and New Zealand Journal of Sociology, 6,* 120–130; Lester, David, Hadley, Richard A., and Lucas, William A. (1990). Personality and a Pro-death Attitude. *Personality and Individual Differences, 11,* 1183–1185.

7. Kalish, Richard A. 1963. Some Variables in Death Attitudes. *The Journal of Social Psychology, 59,* 137–145.

8. Brennan, William J. 1986. Constitutional Adjudication and the Death Penalty: A View from the Court. *Harvard Law Review, 100,* 313–331.

9. Marshall, Thurgood. 1986. Remarks on the Death Penalty Made at the Judicial Conference of the Second Circuit. *Columbia Law Review, 86,* 1–8.

10. Ellsworth, Phoebe C. and Ross, Lee. 1983. Public Opinion and Capital Punishment: A Close Examination of the Views of Abolitionists and Retentionists. *Crime and Delinquency, 29,* 116–169.

11. Roe, Kathleen M. 1989. Private Troubles and Public Issues: Providing Abortion amid Competing Definitions. *Social Science and Medicine, 29,* 1191–1198.

CONNECTED SOLUTIONS

12

Activists Reminisce: An Oral History of Pro-lifers for Survival

The following phone conversation took place on September 29, 2005. Laughter is not recorded but was abundant. The recording was edited for greater clarity and conciseness. The participants were Rachel MacNair, Juli Loesch Wiley, Mary Meehan, and Mary Rider.

Rachel: Let's start with Juli, when you were giving the nuclear energy talk.

Juli: It's a famous story. I was doing atomic Tupperware parties, talking to people in their living rooms and in small groups about nuclear weapons and nuclear power. I made a point of talking about how nuclear radiation would affect particularly the next generation. A woman, who shall forever be called blessed, asked me, "If it's wrong to injure these kids with iodine-131 accidentally, why isn't it wrong to kill them deliberately with curettes?" She was confronting me on abortion, and I didn't have an answer. She was direct and persistent enough that it stayed in my conscience a long time and really challenged me to take all direct assaults on the innocent seriously. The fact that a person in a small group can press a serious question has a power that cannot be denied.

Rachel: Would each of you like to say how you became involved?

Mary Meehan: I believe Juli contacted me about an op-ed piece I had written for the *Washington Post*, asking why there weren't more peace people at the 1979 March for Life. She invited me to attend a big antinuke march in Washington and to help leaflet there. We did that, and one thing led to another. About a dozen of us got together at the 1979 National Right to Life Convention. We decided to leaflet folks who were demonstrating against pro-lifers there.

Juli: As I remember, the Three Mile Island nuclear accident happened in March 1979. In May, they did a huge antinuclear march, and we went to that. We had talked with or had a beer with people in the peace movement we knew were pro-life, and got about nine of us to hand out about 50,000 leaflets.

Mary Meehan: It was a good beginning, and people were friendly.

Juli: It was great. It was a beautiful day, and a couple of the pro-abortion peaceniks came up and sort of listlessly told us that we weren't allowed to leaflet. We remarked that we hadn't seen the newspaper that morning and hadn't realized that the Bill of Rights had been rescinded. They sort of said, "Oh, you assholes!" and walked listlessly away. That was 1979 and was the antinuclear power movement mostly.

But then Reagan became president in 1980, and the Left switched into an antinuclear weapons movement again. I felt energized by that, because to me nuclear weapons and abortion were perfect bookends, symmetrical images of each other. They both involved a frank commitment to targeting innocent targets, and they both depended on the calculated willingness to destroy them deliberately. Looking at it from a reasonable definition of murder—the deliberate killing of innocent persons—it was to me not debatable. I mean, it was not like nuclear power which had calculable risks that could be compared against other risks. Or even conventional war, which can have degrees of limitation, which makes a just war preferable to an unjust peace. The two issues struck me as being so absolute, they set up a kind of a north and south pole—a whole magnetic force that drew in a lot of other issues because of the clarity of those two.

Rachel: But the Mobilization for Survival of Boston didn't see it that way. I remember when Pro-lifers for Survival tried to join the Mobilization for Survival. The Boston Chapter sent out a letter, very exercised about the prospect. Do you remember that?

Juli: Oh, yes! They offered to dismantle the entire Mobilization for Survival if we contaminated them by our membership. They were willing to destroy their movement rather than allowing in this tiny pro-life entity. Evidently they thought pro-"choice" was more important than survival of the planet.

Rachel: I remember at the time thinking the Communist Party has front groups that are members of this coalition. The whole point of having a coalition is that you set aside disagreements on other things to focus on the one thing.

Juli: Exactly. I would have been willing to march beside hot and cold running Trots [Trotskyites] to stop the nuclear arms race. But that kind of latitude was not permitted.

Mary Meehan: Well, there was a debate at the Mobe [Mobilization for Survival] convention in Pittsburgh, remember that? Later, they let me write a little piece against their taking a position on abortion at all, and someone else wrote one saying they should. I think we did at least get some people to take another look at it. I guess they never accepted PS [Pro-lifers for Survival] as a member. Or did they?

Juli: Oh, no.

[Coeditor Stephen Zunes notes, "There were then over 200 member organizations, which makes the upset about PS's application all the more ludicrous. Also, my recollection—I was on the national staff of Mobe at the time and was PS's strongest advocate among them—was that Juli withdrew their application rather than split the organization, so the application was neither formally accepted or rejected.]

Rachel: I remember a memorable line from the Boston letter: *all* pro-lifers are "racist, classist, misogynist, antichoice reactionaries." We set it to music and put it on T-shirts: "Another Racist, Classist, Misogynist, Antichoice Reactionary for Peace."

Juli: Yes. The sad thing is when that faction of the Left sinks its fangs into the peace movement, they sink their fangs and claws and suck the life out of it. They take the peace camp and the peace T-shirts and peace sandals and put them on. So you think you have a peace movement, and what you really have is a raving Left movement that's dressed itself up to look like a peace movement. Because the people who have really thought long and hard about the spiritual, psychological, and social requirements of nonviolence are repelled by them, and yet those are the people who ought to *be* the peace movement.

Mary Meehan: I saw the antiwar march in Washington last weekend, and I saw some of the same hard-edge stuff that's always bothered me. But I also saw some very deeply committed, and probably decades-long-committed peace people.

Rachel: What hops to my mind is how many peace movement people wouldn't consider the pro-life movement because of how turned off they were by people like Jerry Falwell, Jesse Helms, and George Bush.

Juli: Oh, sure. Most people, myself included, when you look at a complicated problem, start off by seeing where your friends are. Because you trust them. There's nothing wrong with that. Your friends are honorable and intelligent people, and you consult them to see what they believe in. But that turns into a camp or culture of the Right or a camp and culture of the Left, not based on real thinking or real dialog—just a desire to move with your particular herd. Us against them, which arouses the most pleasurable, pervasive, and vile passions.

Rachel: And is exactly what the peace movement knows better than to do.

Juli: Yes. It was wonderful to have an organization like Pro-lifers for Survival for a while that tried to respect both of those cultural camps, and understand them, and listen to them, and to act winsomely. Is that a word?

Mary Meehan: It is, a good one.

Juli: To act winsomely towards both sides to talk about serious issues that concern all of us in our hearts and souls.

Mary Meehan: The way everyone hunkers down into political camps—hasn't that been our main problem all along, trying to get a consistency message through?

Mary Rider: If you ever mention in a meeting of left-wing people or right-wing people that you're considering not voting, because you can't compromise your moral standards, the group gets upset you wouldn't do this very important thing. But if you're consistently pro-life, you can't really do that very important thing. If it's that important, when you're voting for one person who is mainly going to be with you on some issues and against you on others, then you're kind of knocking yourself out.

It just doesn't end. I haven't found any consistently pro-life candidates. So you have people who are themselves consistently pro-life, but who decide this is the one issue they'll vote on or this is one they won't vote on. I think we get so caught up in the politics, we forget that that's not the only part of the world where we can effect change. We might be able to effect a lot more change in other parts of society without having to compromise ourselves in the same way.

Mary Meehan: Consistent ethic people who do go into politics, which I think is very important, can do a lot if they focus more on lobbying or coalitions as opposed to electoral politics.

Rachel: Mary Rider, could you talk some about how you became involved?

Mary Rider: I was in junior high when *Roe v. Wade* was passed. My parents were involved in Birthright and Birth Choice. A woman from our church was going to some abortion clinic to protest. I asked my parents if I could go, and they said, "OK." That began my activism. Fast-forward to college, when I was getting ready to graduate and thinking about what to do with this degree in computer science. How was I going to use it outside the military-industrial complex? My mother cut this clip out of the *North Carolina Catholic* that talked about Pro-lifers for Survival and Juli. I guess Juli came through North Carolina on a speaking tour around 1982 or 1983.

So I wrote to Juli, and she sent me a newsletter. An ad said they were looking for organizers and office people. I wrote Juli a letter, and she wrote back, "You can be the Midwest Regional Organizer and move to Chicago." And I said, "Oh, my God! Why would I want to do that?"

Rachel: For the huge amount of money she was offering, right?

Mary Rider: Room and board and ten dollars a week. So I wrote her back. And I said to God, "OK, you're the boss, but I'll let you know I'd rather not go to Chicago." I guess Juli and God got together. She wrote back to me and said, "I've decided to move the national office to Chapel Hill, North Carolina and maybe you could move to Chapel Hill." And I was living in Greenville, North Carolina. So I did.

Rachel: Why Chapel Hill?

Mary Rider: Actually, it wasn't Chapel Hill, it was Hillsborough. There was a woman there who was going to be the office manager, so we got this apartment in this little complex across the street from a jail, and she and I were living there. Then Sheila Short was going to come down from Canada to be with us. Only, she had trouble getting across the border. The first woman was having some family troubles, and things just didn't work out for her. So I ended up moving down the road to Chapel Hill, literally on the same road. Then Juli came down and helped me get some things set up, and we went up to the big march in Washington, the anniversary march of the Poor People's March planned by Martin Luther King. So Juli and I went up there and got together with folks at the Dorothy Day House Catholic Worker and leafleted that march and got things going. Eventually Sheila got across the border and came on down to Chapel Hill and worked as our office manager for a year or two.

This was at the same time that Scott Rains, who was in Syracuse, started doing some regional work up there. After a year or so, his wife, Patti Narcisso, came on board and started editing the newsletter. So eventually they decided it made the most sense to come to Chapel Hill where we could consolidate the office. I was the co-coordinator with Scott of Pro-lifers for Survival for three years. That was approximately August of 1983 to August of 1986. Then I went to graduate school, and Scott and Patti kept things going for another year. Then we had the big conference out of which the Seamless Garment Network was born. That was in 1987 in Chapel Hill.

Juli: The difficulty always is getting adequate officers, leaders, regional leaders, and so forth. You always get people who are committed, but committed to one bank or the other of the river. But not free to let go of either bank and get committed to the bridge in the middle. They would be strongly sympathetic, but were already eaten up with commitments on one end or the other of the dialog.

Mary Rider: I suspect that's what happened, because there was a year actually between Juli and me when John Cavanaugh-O'Keefe and Harry Hand took over things for a while. I know that John is personally a pacifist and was a conscientious objector to the Vietnam War. I think they both were very sympathetic to the idea of "no nukes," but their real work and heart lay in pro-life activism. Once they handed over the reins to me, they went on with the Pro-life Nonviolent Action Project.

The first thing I did with Pro-lifers for Survival was ride down to Orlando with John and Harry to the National Right to Life Convention. That would have been in 1983. We had a Pro-lifers for Survival table there, handing out literature and talking with people. Later they went to the Pax Christi national conventions and had workshops. I presented workshops at those conventions, I think, in San Antonio and again in Erie. And Juli, you may have done some workshops with them, too, because of your roots with Benedictines for Peace.

Juli: That's right. I had been a member of a group called the Pax Center in Erie, Pennsylvania, since 1972. That was the mother, so to speak, of Pax

Christi USA. I was one of the founding members of the Pax Center. Then the Pax Center gave birth, so to speak, to Pax Christi USA, which for a long time has had an official pro-life stand. They didn't *do* much with that stand other than pass a resolution. I hoped for some commitment of time, staff, money, publications, publicity—the kind of networking that generally shows the extent of your commitment. There wasn't much of that. However, they were always hospitable to pro-lifers who wanted to take the initiative and have the literature table or a presence, and they enabled us more than twice to give talks at workshops. That became a kind of institutional home base for us.

Mary Rider: You had your office there for a while too, didn't you?

Juli: It was in the Pax Center in Erie. That was a very hospitable relationship, which I'm grateful for because I don't think it was always easy. I think there were stresses and conflicts about how much time or attention people were supposed to pay to one issue or another. Sister Mary Lou Kownacki, who was the head of the Pax Center for a long time, was always very open and hospitable.

And Sister Joan Chittister, who has a well-deserved reputation for being a thoroughgoing feminist within the Church, was also friendly towards our goals, although she rarely spoke against abortion. She was much criticized by many other feminists for never speaking in favor of it. So Chittister was an interesting and quirky ally and probably in her own way kept the door open with other groups on the Catholic Left by making it seem plausible that you could be a feminist and not be in favor of abortion.

Mary Rider: And she in fact was a signer of the Seamless Garment Network mission statement.

Juli: Yes. And Chittister, of course, was very strong on peace issues.

Rachel: One of my questions is about adventures going in the opposite direction—pro-lifers that were upset about your existence.

Juli: My own spotty memory is that although we got criticism—sometimes people would say, "You don't belong here, you're piggybacking off of our movement with your ban the bomb, not the baby stand"—we didn't really face that much institutional opposition. We *did* have our literature table at National Right to Life and we *were* invited speakers at National Youth Pro-life Coalition conventions. And we did get a chance to do workshops and sessions with pro-life youth groups. Often with sponsorship of their Catholic school, or not just Catholics, even Evangelical colleges, for instance, might have pro-life groups and we'd be invited sometimes to give talks. So it seems, oddly enough, that there was more institutional openness by pro-lifers to accept us as peaceniks than there was vice versa, although I might be wrong. Anyone else want to chime in here?

Rachel: One of the things at the time was that pro-lifers had a strong single-issue orientation. So from their point of view, it's good, we have a group of pro-life lawyers; good, we have a group of pro-life Presbyterians; good, we have a group of pro-life peaceniks. I think the single-issue people understood what coalitions were for. But there were multi-issue groups, like Moral Majority, and columnists like Cal Thomas and Joseph Sobran. Wasn't there more hostility there?

Mary Meehan: I don't remember any from those two but certainly Joe Scheidler and Jim McFadden were pretty outspoken. But I think their problem came not so much with PS but when Cardinal Bernardin started speaking a lot about the consistency ethic. I think their reaction was based not just on what he was saying at the time but on years of frustration with the Catholic hierarchy over the best approaches to winning the pro-life issue. And a feeling on their part, which I think was justified, was that a lot of bishops and clergy really weren't interested in helping the pro-life movement. There was an enormous amount of frustration there. A lot of internal Catholic Church things impeded the consistency ethic as expressed by Cardinal Bernardin. Although, on the other hand, you had people like Nat Hentoff who were immensely attracted by it. I don't think there was hostility to PS as such. It was more the Catholic bishops.

Mary Rider: I think the hardest-core activists on either side felt their commitment was to that one particular thing. The antiabortion folks were willing to say, as long as you're with us on this, we don't care what else you do. And maybe that's as you were saying, Rachel, because it really was more single-issue than the antinuke movement.

One time, I was marching in the March for Life on January 22nd. Our banner said, "Nukes, like knives, abort." This woman got very upset and came up and screamed in my face, "You don't belong here. You're trying to water this down. You're trying to steal away the focus. Get out of here." It was a real challenge. She was literally in my face screaming, she was so upset that I marched with this banner. Of course, that's only one woman. Some people were more challenged by this idea that we might want to work on more things than one at a time.

Mary Meehan: And then some vehemently disagreed with us on the antinuke, antiwar position. I'm not sure over the years we did nearly enough in trying to frame objections to war and the death penalty in terms conservatives would be more simpatico with. There are some very strong conservative arguments against the death penalty. Christopher Derrick did that marvelous short piece on why conservatives should be against war.[1]

Similarly, some people are very good at expressing opposition to abortion and euthanasia in liberal or radical terms. Wesley Smith, for example, has pointed to certain class differences on euthanasia.[2] Pro-euthanasia folks tend to be what he calls the "overclass," not concerned about what euthanasia can do to poor people who have no health care or money.

Mary Rider: There are many folks who, as you were saying, feel this is watering down the antiabortion cause. To bring in other issues is watering down, or we're not really sincere in opposing abortion. We're just saying that to get people to do other things. I would hope, when I was "cattle prodded" in front of an abortion clinic for not moving, I was sincere.

Rachel: Here's an irony: I keep bringing this up with the Consistent Life Board of Directors, and many don't catch it. The reason they don't catch it is, they're spending their time making the pro-life case to peaceniks. So they don't catch what pro-lifers are saying about the consistent life ethic. I mean, isn't that ironic?

Juli: Very much so. Another level of complexity and frustration is the relationship between religious and secular thinkers, religious and secular groups. People deeply involved in moral issues often find that their strongest motivation is the desire to please God. They frame arguments in religious terms. It works well when talking to similar people. They go to the same church, read the same publications, have the same strong central core of motivation. But it renders you almost incomprehensible to people outside that camp. Either way—people who scrupulously disinfect every discourse from any reference to transcendent or religious values also sound incomprehensible to people who pray every day.

Rachel: Do you all remember getting some support from unexpected quarters?

Juli: My unexpected support came from the elder Brent Bozell. He was, I guess, the most right-wing person I've ever met. He was married to Pat Buckley, Bill Buckley's sister, but he broke with the Buckley family because they were too liberal. He was like a monarchist. He thought the last hope on earth was to have a Catholic monarch in Spain. He was sympathetic to political parties that pretty much wanted to install the Catholic code of canon law right there in the Constitution. He was as far Right as he could go without falling off the edge of the earth.

He came to see me one snowy night in the early 1980s. He drove through a snowstorm from Washington, DC, to Erie, Pennsylvania, nonstop because he wanted to talk to me about nuclear arms. He thought nuclear arms were an abomination. Not just the increasingly aggressive kinds of nuclear tactical devices that were being brought online by the Reagan administration and not just the theory of nuclear deterrence but even the mere possession of nuclear weapons, he thought was a mortal sin. And this is a guy who took very seriously the concept of mortal sin. He talked with me for like an hour. He had just driven many hours to talk to me. He sat and talked to me for an hour, stoked up on coffee, on how frustrated he felt that people didn't take the fear of God seriously. And if you threaten, if you possess these diabolical things you could compare it to the possession of hardcore pornography and other things that simply as property don't deserve to exist. He said some kinds of property don't have a right to exist.

Mary Meehan: Like instruments of torture.

Juli: Instruments of torture, nuclear bombs, or suction machines. I was astounded. He was a complex and conflicted man in many ways. A source of his suffering I think was that he did not find people like himself who were princes against contraception and secularism and liberalism, who agreed about the nuclear weapons. Although there were a few. But discovering him was to me was like discovering a new planet in the solar system. I predicted that there would be somebody like that out there, way at the edge of the solar system, orbiting in really big orbits. I had never actually seen one until he appeared at my door.

Rachel: Anybody else have memories of unexpected support?

Mary Meehan: I remember being absolutely delighted in the early 1980s when Nat Hentoff started writing about the Baby Doe cases.[3]

Rachel: And he is agnostic isn't he? An agnostic Jew?

Mary Meehan: Atheist, actually.

Juli: Yeah, he's an atheist. The wonderful thing about it is that people on the Left do respect him despite his odd alliance with unborn babies.

Mary Meehan: His wife was giving him a hard time, and there were people at the *Village Voice* who stopped talking to him. But he's pretty feisty. He can take it.

Juli: One of the odd things, I mean discouraging things, about the fact that abortion has been legal and in certain circles socially acceptable for the last thirty years, is that it does seduce people into supporting infanticide, suicide, voluntary euthanasia, involuntary euthanasia—all those other medical-moral horrors—because of the fact that they are all so congruent with abortion. Good liberals used to always be against killing crippled children. It was unthinkable to talk about giving all those people in the nursing home a lethal overdose of morphine in the name of compassion.

Mary Meehan: That's a source of disappointment to me. I had hoped an emphasis on eugenics would get some liberals to wake up. So much comes from the deep eugenics influence in a lot of organizations, ranging from the American Society of Human Genetics to Planned Parenthood. Katharine O'Keefe, John Cavanaugh O'Keefe's sister, put me onto that back in the early 1990s. I thought, "Great! Here's something liberals are looking into." But to my dismay, most of them haven't.

Mary Rider: I think most of them chose not to. They don't want to know.

Juli: Although typically, pro-lifers are called single-issue on abortion, actually almost all pro-lifers take in at least four medical-moral issues, each one of which is a biggy. That's abortion, infanticide, euthanasia, and suicide. And then, often embryonic human experimentation, which makes the fifth issue. Whereas people in the peace movement tend to do peace movement, death penalty, torture, and sometimes things like prisons or criminal law reform. And of course, poverty. So you don't really have single issues. You really have clusters. All of which throw light on each other.

It's interesting for me, and kind of humbling, to think of an issue like torture. I always thought, "Torture? Everybody's against it. Nobody could be pro-torture." Then people parse it in strange ways. First, "Define torture," and second, "Maybe this is felony abuse but not torture. Or sort of being tortured. Maybe torture is not really torture, it's just a kind of interrogation technique." Or, "You've got to be reasonable about how we handle these dangerous people in confinement."

You get this sudden backing off from even wanting to look at it. A reaction very much like not even wanting to look at abortion—you know—"Don't show me those pictures. It's insulting, it's abusive, it's emotionally manipulative."

Mary Meehan: They just don't want to see them. Well, don't you think compassion fatigue is a factor? It's hard enough to deal with any one of these earth-shaking, deadly serious issues. But to have to deal with all of them at the same time, as most of us tried to do, is a recipe for depression. Don't you think that's one reason people don't want to look at some of those issues?

Juli: I think it is. For sure, I don't want to read about current abuses, because I've got enough. I don't want to think about it.

On the other hand, one of the great ploys and pleasures of being involved in moral issues is the luxury of moral indignation, which leaves me entirely clean and the other side entirely dirty. I can imagine that I myself am so morally perfect; I have no flaws and I and my friends and my political allies are not guilty of anything. Anyone who says any of us are guilty of anything, it's a lie and an exaggeration. It's spin; it's misinformation; it's bad reporting; it's exaggeration. In other words, there are all these reasons why I and my allies could not be guilty of anything *really* seriously wrong. Because it deprives me of the poison pleasure of classifying myself amongst the angels while everybody else falls short by various different degrees. That's hard to get past. Because I know that moral indignation is a very exciting passion for me. It's better than sex.

Mary Rider: Are you putting that in, Rachel?

Rachel: This will be edited. But one thing is that, while all these issues are connected—Daniel Berrigan made this point—the solutions are also connected. That means if you do *any* work on *any* piece of it, it gets around to all the others.

Mary Meehan: That's a very comforting thought, and we probably should hear it more often.

Mary Rider: I'm glad you said that, because sometimes it feels like I do nothing. What have I been doing all these years? How have I made any effect on any of these issues by focusing on all of them? I have to go through this in my head: Yes, we have to work individually on issues, because we have to be specific and have actual answers, not just pointing out problems. But one of the ways we work on the issues is by drawing the connections and trying to help people see that they are connected by the violence they inflict on people. So the solutions are also connected. They must involve a different way of looking at people and valuing people.

NOTES AND REFERENCES

1. Derrick, Christopher. September 1981. Bombs and Babies: Three Baffling Questions. *New Oxford Review*, 3.
2. Smith, Wesley J. 1997. *Forced Exit*. New York: Times Books/Random House, pp. 9–10.
3. Nat Hentoff tells the story for himself in Chapter 3.

13

Activism Throughout the Centuries

Mary Krane Derr

Mary Krane Derr coedited the book ProLife Feminism: Yesterday and Today.[1]

Despite their enduring challenge that antiabortionists show as much concern for the already born as for the unborn, some American pro-choicers react skeptically and dismissively toward the consistent life ethic (CLE). Witness the criticisms of one CLE advocate: "Where he once argued for a confrontation with the pervasive forces of patriarchy, he now argues for a 'seamless garment of life'... now eats at the table of the cultural elite when once he supped with those most marginalized in his community."[2] Despite his self-identification as a "progressive prolife evangelical," he adulates Catholic bishops and their "so-called consistent ethic of life."[3]

Such statements are heavily laden with an all-too-familiar stereotype of abortion opponents—no matter the context, motivations, or import of their beliefs—as sectarian, antiprogressive, misogynist imposers of so-called morality. Yet a "seamless garment of life" can itself be a "confrontation with the pervasive forces of patriarchy," a "supping with those most marginalized." The CLE has long been, and still is, an organically arising, rather than coerced, aspiration among people of diverse faiths and none—not only in history, but *herstory*.

"SEAMLESS GARMENT"

Today in the United States, the idea of a "seamless garment" ethic is generally traced back to the 1980s, when the late Joseph Bernardin, Chicago's Roman

Catholic cardinal, began urging a coherent ethical and political approach to such issues as war, nuclear weaponry, the death penalty, poverty, abortion, and active euthanasia (direct killing, as opposed to letting die). He insisted that such issues be addressed under a seamless garment ethic of respect for all human life. Decades earlier, the Quaker poet/activist Sarah Norcliffe Cleghorn (1876–1959) had applied the Christian Bible's image of the seamless robe to a comprehensive ethic of loving kindness toward both human and animals.[4] Cleghorn was involved in the suffrage, peace, antilynching, child welfare, prison reform, death penalty abolition, socialist, antivivisection, and vegetarian movements. She applauded the original Parliament of the World's Religions (1893). Although her abortion stance (if any) awaits further research, chances are good that many today would find it a surprise (I will soon show why).

Did Bernardin know about this Quaker feminist and her seamless garment ethic? That is not known. However, the term "seamless garment of life" is being gradually supplanted with the more inclusive term "consistent life ethic." Bernardin called for the right of religiously motivated persons and institutions to speak and act in the public sphere, while cautioning them to limit themselves for the good of maintaining a secular state in a pluralistic society. This meant that any religiously grounded positions introduced into the public arena must concern the public good, and must be expressible, and expressed, in terms of the secular society's shared ethical basis.[5]

THE GLOBAL ETHIC

Bernardin was deeply engaged with interfaith dialogue, including the 1993 Parliament of the World's Religions where the unprecedented document *Towards a Global Ethic* was drafted.[6] It articulates "a minimum basic consensus on values and norms" that derives from the teachings of the various religions, yet is one which nonreligious persons can recognize as valid. It is "not some kind of negotiated agreement between the religions, but is a discovery and proclamation of agreements that already exist."[7] The Global Ethic's profoundly shared values and norms are quite ancient yet vitally necessary to live out as ever. Among them are commitments to "a culture of nonviolence and respect for life" and "of equal rights and partnership between men and women."

People from widely diverse religious and cultural backgrounds endorsed the Global Ethic, Bernardin among them. While acknowledging the difficulties of achieving consensus on many disputes, the Declaration asserts that "suitable solutions should be attainable in the spirit of the fundamental principles we have jointly developed here."

What might the Global Ethic mean for the increasingly globalized abortion war? Does it invite the partisans to let go of the curiously shared assumption that their ethics and politics are necessarily, by definition, wholly antithetical to those of "the enemy"? Perhaps, for one, the Global Ethic can disarm the reflexive dismissal of a pro-life or antiabortion position as a misogynist, purely sectarian imposition. Rather, a space for a genuine inquiry can open up: Is this position motivated by genuine respect for fetal life, in a context of active reverence for all life, including female life and sexuality? If so, then it is at the very least compatible with the norms and values of the Global Ethic and open to questions within its Earth-sized parameters.

A WOMAN-AFFIRMING CONSISTENT LIFE ETHIC GOES DEEP

A woman-affirming CLE, like the Global Ethic, is nothing entirely new. The ancient past holds some intriguing hints of such a CLE, even though today they are not always easy to read. History, after all, is written by the "victors." In many times and places, aspirants to respect for all life have proved deeply challenging to entrenched social hierarchies, incurring every sort of negative reaction, from ridicule to execution and getting struck off the historical record.

The ancient Greek mathematician, musician, vegetarian, and spiritual teacher Pythagoras (580 BCE) taught a nonviolence ethic rooted in the kinship of all living beings. Pythagoras's ethic did not exclude or denigrate women. Most unconventionally, Pythagoras defined only sexual misconduct, not intercourse itself, as polluting. He accepted women equally as his students.

Women originally created the Eleusinian Mysteries, and today these rituals deeply fascinate feminist goddess spirituality devotees. According to local custom, celebrants did not sacrifice a victim to the goddess but offered her grapes, other cultivated fruits, honeycombs, and wool. The women had a special feast of grains, with perhaps a little fish. Although today's vegetarians or vegans may find fault here, these rituals were certainly more peaceful and life-affirming than those added on following the Athenian occupation. The Mysteries were changed to begin in Athens with pig and other animal sacrifices. These changes suited Athens's ruling elite, who regularly devoured multicourse flesh meals, considering sow's womb after (induced?) miscarriage to be a delicacy. They ranked women as little better than animals.[8]

Although his legacy has literally come down to us in fragments, a direct contribution of the Pythagorean ethic does remain a cultural presence: the Hippocratic Oath. Some life-respecting provisions of the Oath are still widely held as integral values of medical practice. For example, the commitments to "do no harm"; to observe confidentiality; and to refrain from sexual abuse of patients, even one's social "inferiors." A single provision, however, has in recent decades occasioned fierce controversy: "I will not give a lethal drug to anyone if I am asked, nor will I advise such a plan; and similarly I will not give a woman a pessary to cause an abortion."

The controversy refers little or not at all to the expansively life-revering ethic in which this provision originated. Some right-to-lifers treat it as an ahistorical mandate requiring instant, uncritical obedience. Thus, they do not apply it to physician-assisted, state-sponsored execution. Some pro-choicers seem similarly unaware of the Pythagorean ethic's character, let alone its resonance with present-day values and norms they may aspire to themselves. Thus they find this provision at best irrelevant today and at worst hostile to sick or disabled persons and women.

In his *Roe v. Wade* ruling, Harry Blackmun states that Pythagoreans, in a "spirit of uncompromising austerity," "frowned upon" suicide and opposed abortion as "a matter of dogma," the "dogma" that "the embryo was animate from the moment of conception, and abortion meant destruction of a living being." He notes the commonplace practice and advocacy of abortion and suicide in the ancient Greco-Roman world. Thus, the Oath's Pythagorean values represent not "an absolute standard for medical conduct," but a minority, sectarian, largely unpersuasive view that survived only because Christians adopted it. Blackmun staunchly defended *Roe* for the rest of his life, despite his famous announcement in a capital punishment case that he has done "tinkering with the machinery of death."[9]

"Frowned upon," "dogma," "uncompromising austerity": Might not Blackmun be projecting a late twentieth-century stereotype of grim, rigid moralizers with peculiar opinions onto people it probably does not fit? And even if a position is in the minority, why and how should that in and of itself invalidate it? Large numbers of Americans have looked with disfavor on death penalty abolitionists like the later Blackmun—yet that by no means invalidates his decision to take up their cause. But what makes Blackmun's concern for life on death row qualitatively different from the Pythagorean or present-day concern for fetal life? What if he had known that Pythagoreans—and other abortion opponents from antiquity to the present—aspired to respect for *all* lives, including women's?

Curiously, Blackmun then concludes, "[A]ncient religion did not bar abortion." Did he mean the state religions of Greece and Rome? These also did not bar—and even outright sanctioned—many practices that today's pro-lifers and pro-choicers alike would likely agree were oppressive and undesirable of repetition. For example, the Roman paterfamilias, or oldest male in the household, legally claimed not only all its property, but *vitae necisque potestas,* the power of life and death over its members, "free" and enslaved. He could force a woman to undergo an abortion or her baby to undergo infanticide. Disability, being of the female gender, or nonmarital birth usually doomed newborns. He could sell displeasing older children into slavery or have them executed. The state made spectacles of violent mass human and animal killings regular public entertainment. Small wonder that Martin Luther King, Jr., offered early Christian resistance to officially sanctioned violence in ancient Rome as a model for the African-American civil rights movement.[10]

Michael Gorman supplies a much fuller context for early Christian opposition to abortion than Blackmun does.[11] Examining the first four centuries of the Common Era, he notes that Christians formed their position *before* negative attitudes toward women and sexuality took official hold. Gorman places early Christians' stance squarely within "a consistent pro-life ethic" that "pleaded for the poor, the weak, women, children, and the unborn" and "discarded hate in favor of love, war in favor of peace, oppression in favor of justice, bloodshed in favor of life." Some early Christians refrained from flesh-eating as well, as many do today.[12]

Unlike Blackmun, Gorman notes the non-Pythagorean influences on the early Christian CLE—notably, Judaism. In the ancient Greco-Roman world, Jews were well known—and mocked—for their countercultural shunning of abortion, infanticide, and suicide. The Jewish scholar Philo of Alexandria argued against abortion by describing the unborn child as being like a sculpture in progress, to be left in the artist's studio until completion. His simile acknowledges women's creative, active, indispensable role in gestation, in contrast to the more popular Aristotelian portrayal of women as passive containers for exclusively male seed.

Judaism, of course, has developed on its own terms, to this very day. This should go without saying, but sadly, it can't: Judaism has its own identity and integrity, regardless of how it has or has not affected Christianity. Since antiquity, Jewish ethics have emphasized the intrinsic sacredness of life. Killing of humans and animals is not permitted except in a relatively few, carefully circumscribed situations, such as self-defense or kosher slaughtering of animals for food or hides only. Vegetarianism, the diet in the Garden of Eden (Genesis 1:21), remains an option, and, in the view of some, the ideal cuisine.[13] The Mishnah, rabbinical Judaism's founding document, teaches that one should hold all lives dear, including disabled people's, and indeed cultivate gratitude for human diversity.[14]

Blackmun mentions that abortion was proscribed in ancient Persia but without mentioning Zoroastrianism, a still-living faith that predated Judaism and Christianity and contributed richly to both. From their beginnings, Zoroastrian ethics have emphasized the spiritual equality of men and women and the human responsibility for ecological caretaking. Zoroastrian scripture presents abortion as an unjust taking of the child's life and reassures a pregnant, unmarried woman that she need not feel shame and thus resort to it. The father and the community also have obligations toward sustaining the child's life, prenatally and postnatally.[15]

Blackmun entirely misses other ancient religions. Oceania's Chamorro people governed their society according to woman-affirming values rooted in their stories of a female Creator. They still apparently lack a word in their language for induced abortion because of its precolonial unthinkability.[16] A highly sophisticated spirituality of *ahimsa*—"nonviolence by all faculties, mental, verbal, and physical . . . compassion for all forms of life"[17] —remains at the heart of Hindu, Jain, and Buddhist ethics, which began well before or during the time of Pythagoras. All three religions have long extended ahimsa to women and embryos alike. Who else did Blackmun not explore?

For all the shortcomings in his account, unfortunately, some pro-choicers, like Lorayne Ray, continue to rely on it and its limited references. Ray finds it "inconceivable" that people as "intelligent" as Pythagoras and his followers could connect the issues of abortion, suicide, and the status of animals—let alone be so "extreme" as to value fetuses. She remarks, "To my knowledge, only a few Hindu religions still believe that souls inhabit animals."[18] Not only is this remark counterfactual, it sounds laden with an assumption (conscious or unconscious) that "non-Western" people are backward and superstitious.

This is the same presumption that assailed Anandibai Joshee over a century ago. She was the first Hindu and the first Asian Indian of either sex to earn a medical doctorate degree in the United States in 1886. Joshee's steadfast vegetarian diet was a contemptible curiosity to heavily meat-eating Americans. In her home country, vegetarianism has been admired for millennia as a sign of advanced spirituality.

To "prove" that Indians were savages in dire need of "civilizing," the British East India Company and Christian missionaries spread the myth that Hinduism encouraged infanticide. Never mind that colonialism had destroyed the social safety net, subjecting Indians to unprecedented levels of poverty and hunger and causing a tremendous rise in infanticide, especially of girls. Joshee dismantled this myth:

> [O]f the mothers who distraught with poverty sometimes throw their babies into the Ganges, Dr. Joshee noted that during her medical experience in Philadelphia a large number of new-born infants, either murdered or deserted, found their way into the dissecting-room. She said she might as well on her return to India relate this fact, making it a *custom* of American mothers to kill or desert their children, and adducing it as a result of Christian belief, as to charge the Hindu faith with the drowning so often reported.[19]

At age fourteen, Joshee had lost her only child ten days after delivery—because, she felt, of the doctor's incompetence. Indeed, infant and maternal mortality were quite high in British-occupied India because of insufficient medical care. Joshee decided to become a physician to spare other mothers and children from preventable suffering. As she studied at the Woman's Medical College of Pennsylvania, she sought to reclaim an advanced Indian obstetrical tradition dating back as far as the fifteenth century BCE. It had become lost under colonialism. In her MD thesis, she describes elements of this tradition that she felt still honored "the value of life and health:" the ability to differentiate the signs of a conception from those of an already established pregnancy; careful daily attentions to protect, "from the time of conception," the lives, health, and peace of the woman and "the child" equally; and the advice to physicians and midwives "that they are but second hands to Nature . . . in her wise work."

She does mention a surgical procedure for dismembering the unborn child during labors complicated by transverse presentation. However, the physician or midwife should first try manually maneuvering the fetus into correct place; the knife should be avoided if the fetus is still alive, although it may "seldom" be necessary.[20] Joshee's attitudes toward the pregnant woman and the fetus express her own personal sensibilities, experiences, and broad compassion as well as Hindu devotion to the sacredness of all lives and the need to refrain from abortion, except as a last resort to preserve the woman's life.[21]

Although it can be difficult to decipher ancient beliefs, as Blackmun himself notes, what might happen if well-qualified scholars cultivated an openness toward the possibilities of a woman-affirming CLE in the ancient past? At the same time, as the example of Joshee's own life and work suggests, it is not necessary to look so far back for one.

PRE-1960s FEMINISM

Whatever its first inklings may have been, a woman-affirming CLE can be discerned, in far more abundant and verifiable detail, throughout the herstory of "modern" feminism, starting at least with Mary Wollstonecraft. If Sarah Cleghorn's seamless robe did in fact enfold unborn children, she was in agreement not only with Bernardin, but the vast majority of pre-1960s feminists. Feminist advocacy of a moral and political right to abortion on "demand" has only taken hold on a wide scale since the 1960s. Yet it rapidly became so entrenched that other feminist positions, both past and present, became forgotten or unthinkable.

Many pro-choice feminists became quite leery of even overlapping with pro-lifers in some regard. By the early 1980s, pro-choice theologian Beverly Harrison was faulting the pro-life pacifist-feminist Juli Loesch for saying that the Latin word "fetus" means "unborn child."[22] This was, insisted Harrison, "a debatable point; Latin dictionaries are treasure troves of 'traditionalist' theological opinion."[23] Yet a mere dozen years before, when the pro-choice *Our Bodies, Ourselves* had debuted in a stapled-paper, 35-cent edition, it had prefaced a full description of prenatal development with an almost identical translation of the Latin word in question.[24]

Not surprisingly, pro-life feminists have found it very difficult to find a hearing, let alone acceptance, among other feminists. Not only is their commitment to and compassion for women subject to denial, if they speak of the CLE in feminist herstory, they may be told that they are manipulative liars pushing some nasty covert agenda. There are of course some thankful exceptions to this pattern. Yet this part of herstory is still largely unmentioned (and unmentionable!). Or, if recognized in the past, it is chalked up to prudery and abhorrence of nonprocreative sex; the procedure's illegality and danger to women; "regular" (allopathic) physicians' drive to eliminate "irregular" (alternative) doctors and midwives as competition; a restrictive, mandatory-motherhood mystique; and/or patriarchal religious dogma.

Early feminists *were* quite concerned about abortion's physical and psychological dangers to women, as indeed any feminist today should be, whatever its legal status. However, they sought to eliminate abortion itself, not to gain legal and ethical sanction for it. Endangerment to women was not their only or even primary objection. Nor was abortion's illegality. Many early feminists committed nonviolent civil disobedience: sheltering runaway slaves and abused wives, refusing to pay taxes, attempting to enter polls and vote, picketing, marching, and providing sexual/reproductive health education and services. Yet they supported disincentives to abortion, even as they devoted themselves primarily to thorough relief of its root causes.

Not all sought to suppress "irregular" doctors and midwives; many early feminists *were* such practitioners or their enthusiastic clients and advocates. The early feminists did celebrate motherhood as a uniquely female power and strength that deserved genuine reverence. They simultaneously exposed the motherhood mystique as a cover-up for real-life degradations and asserted through their words and deeds that not every woman had to be a literal mother. Recognizing that women had creative capacities other than the womb's, early feminists fought for women's entrance into higher education and the professions, resisting the dictum that female physiology inherently prevents public achievement.

Their perspectives on motherhood led naturally to their outspoken resistance to prudery and the sexual double standard. Many affirmed the value of sex for pleasure and communication, not just procreation, for both sexes. They actively promoted sexual and reproductive health education, male responsibility, and "voluntary motherhood" as urgently necessary alternatives to abortion, along with direct service and public policy aid to pregnant women and other mothers. All of them agreed that abstinence was a valid means of exercising the right to voluntary motherhood, also called the "right over one's own body." A number of them extended that right to prolonged breastfeeding, withdrawal, coitus reservatus, douches, condoms, pessaries (which evolved into diaphragms), and the earliest forms of fertility awareness/natural family planning. Some also sanctioned the sexual practices now called outercourse. Until the early twentieth century, rise of eugenic homophobia sent many GLBT persons back into the closet. Some feminists, like Drs. Emily Blackwell and Elizabeth Cushier, openly chose "Boston marriages," lifetime domestic partnerships between women. Early feminists worked for women's right to choose pain relief during labor, to have trained, skilled midwifery services, and to avoid unnecessary, overly aggressive surgical and medical interventions.

For their courageous, plainspoken advocacy of nonviolent choice, many early U.S. feminists ran afoul of Anthony Comstock, the antivice crusader and book burner who gave his name to the federal antiobscenity statute in

1873, equating sexual/reproductive health education with pornography, family planning with abortion, and abortion with "sexual immorality" *instead* of life-taking. Comstock boasted of driving at least fifteen "enemies" to suicide.

Patriarchal, sectarian religious dogma was not an early feminist motive either. Pre-1960s feminism brought together women from diverse faiths with freethinkers—people seeking spirituality outside organized religion, or identifying themselves as theosophists, agnostics, or atheists. Feminists of faith, like their other-than-religious sisters, critically questioned and challenged injustice-promoting doctrines as an integral part of their devoted service to womankind and humankind.

What motive might be left for early feminists' opposition to abortion? Their terminology does speak for itself. They repeatedly called the procedure "antenatal murder," "child murder," "antenatal infanticide," or simply "infanticide." They spoke of *two* lives being lost in any abortion that killed both the woman and fetus. They regarded abortion as a violent wrong against *women* as well, one arising from the violent wrong of denying women authentic sexual and reproductive choices.

In *Herland*, Charlotte Perkins Gilman's vegetarian, ecofeminist utopia, a confounded male explorer asks one of its citizens how they so successfully control their reproduction. He adds, "You surely do not destroy the unborn." With a look of "ghastly horror" on her face, the woman "starts from her chair, pale, her eyes blazing." She whispers, "Destroy the unborn!—Do men do that in your country?"[25] Yet early feminists did not consider horror over abortion something to reserve for a utopian future; it had to be made unthinkable immediately.

SHAPING THE EARLY FEMINIST APPROACH

This early feminist approach was shaped by recent scientific discoveries about conception and prenatal development; Mary Wollstonecraft's groundbreaking life and work; the egalitarianism of the Haudenosaunee Six Nations; the antislavery movement; and women's poignant "heart-histories" around sexual and reproductive issues.

Until the early nineteenth century, "Western" science did not know that the life of each human organism commenced with the union of one female and one male cell. Women found this new information empowering. It challenged Aristotle's theory of the male seed as the active, animating principle and the woman as passive container. Feminist sexual/reproductive health educators democratized the new scientific knowledge, teaching eager women the facts about conception, prenatal development, and women's indispensable role in pregnancy. Lucinda Banister Chandler urged that the law stop "perpetuat[ing] one of the errors of barbarism which science is exploding and experience is constantly disproving, viz., that the father alone is the creative power."[26]

Though berated for her visionary ideas and her single motherhood, Mary Wollstonecraft inspired feminists in and beyond Britain, largely through her 1792 book, *Vindication of the Rights of Woman* (parodied, tellingly, as *Vindication of the Rights of Brutes,* that is, animals). In this book, she advocates voluntary, woman-controlled family planning, while opposing abortion and infanticide. As a result of male exploitation,

> [w]omen becoming consequently weaker, in mind and body, than they ought to be, have not sufficient strength to discharge the first duty of a mother; and... either destroy the embryo in the womb, or cast it off when born... [M]en ought to maintain the women they have seduced....[27]

Many of the earliest Euro-American suffragists were connected to upstate New York, among whom were the great "suffrage triumvirate" of Elizabeth Cady Stanton, Susan B. Anthony, and Matilda Joslyn Gage, and their beloved elder, Lucretia Mott. The area's Native Americans, the Haudenosaunee Six Nations (whom the French called Iroquois), tremendously inspired them. Haudenosaunee women enjoyed remarkable freedom in matters of sex, motherhood, property, marriage, divorce, work, religion, and government.[28] The Haudenosaunee religion's Code of Handsome Lake cautions against environmental devastation, domestic violence, child abuse, the stigmatization of nonmarital pregnancies, and abortion, regarded as unjust fetal life-taking that hurts women, too.[29]

The U.S. feminist movement also grew from the slavery abolition movement. Black and white women discerned strong parallels between gender and race oppression, but threatening mobs and abolitionist men alike opposed their public actions. Yet Angelina and Sarah Grimké, daughters of a slave plantation owner, documented black women's sexual and reproductive traumas anyway.[30] Sarah identified men's property claims over women as a prime cause of abortion and the right to voluntary motherhood as a safeguard against it.

> Has [woman] not, too often, when thus compelled to receive the germ she could not welcome, refused to retain & nourish into life the babe which she felt was not the fruit of a pure connubial love?... Surely as upon her alone devolves the necessity of nurturing unto the fullness of life the being within her & after it is born... she ought to have the right of controlling all preliminaries.[31]

The pressures upon slave women like Margaret Garner toward abortion, infanticide, and suicide deeply distressed feminists. In 1858, as a fugitive slave facing capture, Garner killed her three-year-old daughter and tried to commit suicide.[32] Harriet Ann Jacobs wrote about her physician "master's" relentless sexual harassment. She tried to resist it through a relationship with another white man whom she "at least did not despise." When Jacobs became pregnant, the "master" angrily denounced her "disgrace" and "ingratitude," reminding her of his power of life and death over her and her unborn child. "He intimated that if I had accepted his proposals, he, as a physician, could have saved me from exposure . . . Could he have offered wormwood more bitter?" Wormwood (the Biblical gall) was a well-known folk abortifacient. More than once, Jacobs contemplated death for herself and her children, never imaging that one day they would escape slavery.[33] The bitter, horrific experiences of women like Garner and Jacobs shaped early feminist portrayals of abortion and infanticide as desperate, violent acts to escape the enslaving conditions imposed on mothers of all backgrounds.

Early feminists engaged very seriously with women's "heart-histories" around sex and reproduction and tapped into their personal and societal healing power. This comes from the practice of pioneering women physicians, whose healing practices included empathetic listening to patients in order to draw out their "heart-histories"—narratives of their own inner experiences and emotions.[34] As happened with Anandibai Joshee and the Grimkés, personal trials and empathetic engagement with other women's experiences brought many into feminist action. Spiritualist minister and free love advocate Laura Cuppy Smith became San Francisco's "radical of radicals" after midwifing her single teen daughter and baby grandson through an unexpected pregnancy and beyond.[35] After evangelical Christian Kate Waller Barrett met a single mother and her child for the first time, she resolved to "wipe out some of the inequities that were meted out to my sisters." She went on to lead a national organization of shelters for pregnant women.[36]

EXPANDING TO ALL

Early feminist concern for unborn children was closely interwoven with care for already-born children and of course for women, among others oppressed and subjected to violence. "The expansion of the definition of life to include the whole career of the fetus rather than only the months after quickening is quite consistent. It was in line with a number of movements to reduce cruelty and to expand the concept of the sanctity of life."[37]

For feminists, it was a matter of respecting actual lives, not simply dealing with an abstract concept. In 1886, feminists protested the much-ballyhooed unveiling of the Statue of Liberty. Why all the fuss over an abstract stone symbol when the flesh-and-blood women's fierce struggles for freedom were still so undermined and neglected? On this occasion, Matilda Joslyn Gage proclaimed, "All the struggles for freedom are connected.... Our struggle is for all life. Liberty is the key to maintaining it."[38]

Early feminists honored female and fetal lives in the context of interrelated human rights and welfare issues and movements that are too many to recount here in any great detail: civil rights for oppressed racial/ethnic groups, peace, anti-imperialism, resistance to genocide, the labor movement, disability rights, children's rights, environmentalism, animal concerns, and vegetarianism. Despite deliberate forgetting, distortion, and censorship, the woman-affirming CLE that characterized pre-1960s feminism has reemerged, persisted, and evolved up to the present day. Its American advocates are reaching out globally and discovering that many women in the Two-Thirds World, like Kenyan ecofeminist and Nobel Peace Prize laureate Wangari Maathai, already hold quite similar views. The automatic equation of antiabortion with sectarian misogyny becomes ever more untenable.

Pro-life and pro-choice ideologies alike aspire toward a world where women have such an abundance of nonviolent choices that abortion is very rare indeed. Opening up the CLE's herstory has the power to show that "the enemy" may not be who one fears. I offer this herstory in the hope that it can move us all a little closer toward an Earth where women can be at peace in their own wombs, an Earth already envisioned for us by openhearted, farseeing foremothers, and even forefathers, before anyone living today was even conceived.

NOTES AND REFERENCES

1. Derr, Mary Krane, Rachel MacNair, and Linda Naranjo-Huebl, eds. 2006. *ProLife Feminism: Yesterday and Today*, 2nd expanded ed. Available through the Feminism & Nonviolence Studies Association, http://www.fnsa.org, or at http://www.xlibris.com/ProLifeFeminism.

2. Payson, Aaron. Summer 2005. The Politics of Jim Wallis. *Conscience*.

3. Kissling, Frances. Autumn 2005. A Cautionary Tale. *Conscience*.

4. Cleghorn, Sarah. 1945. *The Seamless Robe: The Religion of Loving kindness*. New York: Macmillan.

5. Bernardin, Joseph. 1988. The Consistent Ethic: What Sort of Framework? In *Abortion and Catholicism: The American Debate*, ed. Patricia Beattie Jung and Thomas A. Shannon. New York: Crossroad.

6. Council for a Parliament of the World's Religions. 1993. *Towards a Global Ethic (An Initial Declaration)*. Chicago: Author.

7. Baima, Thomas. How to Read *The Declaration toward a Global Ethic*. In Joel Beversluis, ed., *A Sourcebook for Earth's Community of Religions*. Grand Rapid, MI: CoNexus Press/New York: Global Education Associates.

8. Adams, Carol J. 1990/1998. *The Sexual Politics of Meat: A Feminist-Vegetarian Critical Theory*. New York: Continuum; Gage, Matilda Joslyn. 1898. *Woman, Church, and State*. Chicago: Charles Kerr; Spencer, Colin. 2000. *Vegetarianism: A History*. New York: Four Walls Eight Windows.

9. Blackmun, Harry. February 22, 1994. Dissenting Opinion in *Callins v. Collins*, United States Supreme Court.

10. King Jr., Martin Luther. April 16, 1963. Letter from a Birmingham Jail.

11. Gorman, Michael J. 1982. *Abortion and the Early Church: Christian, Jewish, and Pagan Views of Abortion in the Greco-Roman World*. Eugene, OR: Wipf & Stock.

12. Christian Vegetarian Association. 2005. Web site: http://www.christianveg.com.

13. Jewish Vegetarians of North America. n.d. Jewish Veg: Our Diet as Kiddush Hashem (Online), http://www.jewishveg.com.

14. Gracer, Bonnie L. Spring 2003. What the Rabbis Heard: Deafness in the Mishnah. *Disability Studies Quarterly* 192–205.

15. Cowasjee, Toxy, ed. 2000. *Daughters of Mashyani Hall of Fame*. Houston, TX: Seventh World Zoroastrian Congress. Archived at Zarathushti/Zoroastrian Women's International Network, http://www.zwin3.net/zynop_401.html; Federation of Zoroastrian Associations of North America (FEZANA). August 15, 2005. Our challenge: Voices for peace, partnership and renewal. Press release by author. Archived at http://www.zagny.org; Jafarey, Ali A. 2005. Woman in the Avesta and the Later Gathas. Zaruthushtrian Assembly Web site: http://www.Zoroastrian.org.

16. Dames, Vivian Loyola. 2003. Chamorro Women, Self-determination, & the Politics of Abortion on Guam. In Shirley Hune and Gail M. Nomura, eds., *Asian/Pacific Islander American Women*. New York: New York University Press.

17. Salgia, Amar T. 1995. Jainism: A Portrait. In Joel Beversluis, ed., *A Sourcebook for Earth's Community of Religions*. Grand Rapids, MI: CoNexus Press/New York: Global Education Associates.

18. Ray, Lorayne. 2003. *What I Told My Daughters about Abortion*. Van Nuys, CA: Enlightened Press.

19. Dall, Caroline Healey. 1888. *The Life of Anandibai Joshee*. Boston: Roberts Brothers.

20. Joshee, Anandibai. 1886. *Obstetrics Under the Aryan Hindoos*. Doctor of Medicine thesis, Woman's Medical College of Pennsylvania.

21. Subramuniyaswami, Sivaya. January 1993. Let's Talk about Abortion. *Hinduism Today*, http://www.hinduismtoday.com/archives/1993/01/1993-01-05.shtml.

22. Loesch, Juli. November 1980. Fetus Is Latin for Unborn Child. *Sojourners Magazine*, p. 19.

23. Harrison, Beverly Wildung. 1983. *Our Right to Choose: Toward a New Ethic of Abortion.* Boston: Beacon Press.
24. Boston Women's Health Course Collective. 1971. *Our Bodies, Ourselves: A Course by and for Women.* Boston: New England Free Press.
25. Gilman, Charlotte Perkins. 1916/1979. *Herland.* New York: Pantheon Books.
26. Leach, William. 1980. True Love and Perfect Union: The Feminist Reform of Sex and Society. New York: Basic Books.
27. Wollstonecraft, Mary. 1792/1975. *Vindication of the Rights of Woman,* ed. Carol Poston. New York: W.W. Norton & Company.
28. Roesch Wagner, Sally. 2001. *Sisters in Spirit: Haudenosaunee (Iroquois) Influence on Early American Feminists.* Summertown, TN: Native Voices.
29. Parker, Arthur Caswell, transl. 1913. *The Code of Handsome Lake, the Seneca Prophet.* Albany: New York State Museum.
30. Weld, Theodore. 1839. *American Slavery as It Is: Testimony of a Thousand Witnesses.* New York: American Anti-Slavery Society.
31. Grimké, Sarah. n.d./1992. Marriage. In Gerda Lerner, ed., *The Female Experience: An American Documentary.* Oxford: Oxford University Press.
32. Coffin, Levi. 1880. *Reminiscences of Levi Coffin.* Cincinnati, OH: Robert Clarke & Company.
33. Jacobs, Harriet. 1861. *Incidents in the Life of a Slave Girl, Written by Herself.* Boston: Privately printed.
34. Wells, Susan. 2001. *Out of the Dead House: Nineteenth Century Women Physicians and the Writing of Medicine.* Madison: Wisconsin University Press.
35. Smith, Laura Cuppy. March 1, 1873/2005. How One Woman Entered the Ranks of Social Reform—Or, a Mother's Story. *Woodhull's and Claflin's Weekly.* Reprinted in Derr, MacNair, and Naranjo-Huebl, *ProLife Feminism: Yesterday and Today.*
36. Kunzel, Regina G. 1993. *Fallen Women, Problem Girls: Unmarried Mothers and the Professionalization of Social Work, 1890–1945.* New Haven, CT: Yale University Press.
37. Degler, Carl. 1980. *At Odds: Women and the Family in America from the Revolution to the Present.* Oxford: Oxford University Press.
38. Roesch Wagner, Sally. 1998. *A Time of Protest.* Aberdeen, SD: Sky Carrier Press.

Changing Hearts and Minds

Mary Meehan

What is it that turns people around on issues of life and death? What leads them to choose life over war, abortion, the death penalty, suicide, and euthanasia? If they are on the "death side" of any of these issues, how can we help them turn around?

It's important to remember that persuasion is an art, not a science. Logic can and should help the process, but human beings are not logic machines. We are complicated critters, with layers of experience, buckets of questions, sudden springs of hope, and many contradictions. All of this works against an approach of sheer logic. Often, we have to touch people's hearts before we can reach their minds. Or perhaps, it's better to say that we have to do both at the same time.

Perhaps you are discussing life issues with a friend or someone you met recently on a trip. It might even be someone who is picketing against your position—someone you befriend on the spot.

MESSENGERS WITH A ZEST FOR LIFE

The messenger may be the most important part of the message. Helen Alvaré, an attorney who for years was a leading pro-life spokeswoman, once said that "people are more or less attracted to your message in direct proportion to whether they are... attracted to your person." She listed several key questions about an audience. "Do they like people like you?... Do they like the world-view you're selling? Do they want to live there?"[1] Alvaré herself was extremely effective as a spokeswoman because she has a zest for life, is attractive and a skilled speaker, and has a good sense of humor. She has pizzazz. But when the time comes for it, she can trade logic with the best of them, and she has deep commitment. We can't all have her talents, but all of us should have a zest for life, a real sense of its joy and adventure. If we communicate that in our speech and behavior, others are inclined, in Alvaré's words, to like the worldview we're selling and "want to live there."

One problem, though, is that some people who are deeply involved in the defense of human life are beaten down by all the threats to life and the great difficulty of overcoming them. They may feel guilty, at least subconsciously, about the idea of enjoying life when so many victims of violence and killing cannot enjoy it. They may sink into depression and become wholly ineffective in their work, because their depression repels the very people they want to convert.

This problem may be more widespread than people realize, in every movement for social change. Nearly all of the battles are uphill and discouraging, so much so that some activists live on the edge of despair for many years. It's important for them to realize that, as W. B. Yeats wrote, "Too long a sacrifice/Can make a stone of the heart."[2] They absolutely need to get away, on a regular basis, from work and worry and deadly serious issues. They need days off and real vacations; time to walk in the woods, visit old friends, take a child on a merry-go-round, or rake leaves in the bracing air of a fine October day; time to do everything that reminds them of why they enlisted to defend life in the first place. Only if they do this, only if they understand that they have a right to "the pursuit of happiness," can they be effective in working for others' lives and chance for happiness.

RESPECT FOR THE PERSON

Respect for others should be a bedrock position of anyone involved in the defense of life, and it includes respect for one's adversaries. This means avoiding personal attacks. It means refraining from name-calling that depersonalizes others by reducing them to a general political stance or to their positions on an issue ("right-wing fanatics" or "the religious right," "leftists" or "pro-aborts"). It's important to stay focused on the *act* of killing rather than personal attacks on those who support it. We can't know their interior state, and we have to remember that good people can support evil acts—and do so in good conscience, although conscience caught in deep error.

In opening doors and hearts, there is no substitute for old-fashioned courtesy. Years ago I saw Elizabeth McAlister and other peace activists leaflet at the

Pentagon during a Good Friday protest against nuclear weapons. The peace supporters were both polite and cheerful; they knew that courtesy does not mean selling out one's convictions. Replying to "Happy Easter!" from one leafleter, a Pentagon worker said, "Thank you. God bless you."

In many cases, of course, the folks on the other side respond with hostility instead of goodwill. Then we have to go deeper than respect and courtesy; we have to go to love. Rev. Dr. Martin Luther King, Jr., managed to do this right after his home was bombed during the Montgomery bus boycott that he led in 1955–1956. King was presiding over a mass meeting in church at the time, but his wife, infant daughter, and a visitor were at the King home. Fortunately, they were not harmed by the bomb, though the house certainly was. Dr. King, alerted about the bombing, rushed to the scene and found his home surrounded by a large and growing crowd of African-Americans who were quite angry about the bombing. City officials and police feared there would be a riot, but King calmed the crowd and urged them to go home. "I want you to love our enemies," he said. "Be good to them. Love them and let them know you love them."[3]

It would be hard for any movement defending life to find a better slogan than this in dealing with its adversaries: *Love them and let them know you love them.*

Some former abortion clinic workers have been won over to the pro-life side because of the love they experienced from people who demonstrated against their clinics. Norma McCorvey, former lead plaintiff as "Jane Roe" in *Roe v. Wade,* is one.[4] The case of another, Judith Fetrow, is striking because she initially experienced hostility from pro-life demonstrators at the Planned Parenthood abortion clinic where she worked. On one occasion, she was so upset by her work that she decided to leave the clinic. But on her way out, demonstrators started shouting at her, "Murderer! The blood is on your hands!" Fetrow felt as though "someone had kicked me in the stomach," so she went back into the clinic and "back to work."

But a sidewalk counselor named Steve reached out to her, chatting with her in a friendly way. "It took some time," Fetrow recalled, "it took enormous dedication, and it took the patience of a saint. But over several weeks we developed a friendship across the lines, based on trust." Fetrow again left the clinic; but this time she did not return.[5]

UNDERSTAND WHERE THEY'RE COMING FROM

When Sister Helen Prejean, C.S.J., was first involved in the anti-death penalty movement, she did not reach out to the families of murder victims. That would have been awkward, since she was serving as spiritual adviser to a man on death row. But Prejean had a virtue that is too rare among activists—she was able to learn from her critics. Some complained in letters to editors that she hadn't contacted the families of the man's victims. So she urged a Catholic bishop to visit and comfort the families of the two victims, who lived in his diocese, and the bishop did so. Prejean also encouraged an acquaintance to involve the diocese in survivors' support work. This resulted in a special annual Mass, led by the bishop, for victims of criminal violence. The diocese also helped organize a victims' support group.

In another case, Vernon Harvey, a murder victim's stepfather who suffered deep grief and a consuming desire for vengeance, contacted Sister Prejean, who offered to visit him and his wife. Prejean was then spiritual adviser to a man on death row who had raped and murdered the Harveys' daughter. Her visit resulted in a friendship with the Harveys, although one subjected to much strain. Prejean attended executions to pray with and comfort the men about to die, while the Harveys were there to celebrate.

It was a rewarding friendship, though, especially after the Harveys invited Prejean to attend a Parents of Murdered Children meeting. Prejean didn't want to go. "I've been avoiding the victims," she admitted to herself, "because I'm afraid they'll turn on me and attack me. I fear their anger and rejection. Plus, I feel so helpless in face of their suffering. I don't begin to know how to help them." But she summoned up the courage to go, and she learned much from the other survivors, as she had from the Harveys. This helped her start a support group for the family survivors of murder victims in New Orleans. It also helped make Prejean's *Dead Man Walking* one of the best anti-death penalty books there is, because it acknowledges the enormity of the crimes that send people to death row, describes the deep suffering of the victims' survivors, and suggests ways to help the survivors.[6]

Antiwar activists would do well to follow Prejean's example by talking to hawkish war veterans and to families of men and women killed in combat. This will not necessarily lead to conversions on either side, but it might result in greater sensitivity on both sides and less bitterness in debates over war. This means that more citizens are likely to listen to the debates and take their substance seriously. Whatever they think of the constitutional aspects of laws against flag-burning, for example, antiwar people should be able to say, "We're just flat-out opposed to burning the flag. Many brave soldiers have suffered greatly and died under that flag. We don't want to dishonor their sacrifice or add to their families' suffering." Likewise, veterans and families of those killed in combat should be able to say about, let's say, the war in Iraq, "Many of us think the antiwar people are mistaken, but we can't question their patriotism. And we know that they mourn the American casualties of this war, as well as the Iraqi ones."

Citizens who contact politicians about life-and-death issues are more effective when they understand where the politicians are coming from. Often it's *not* just politics, as we're too likely to assume. Many politicians have had personal experiences that bear on the issue at hand. Some members of the Congress, for example, are war veterans. It's helpful to know about their war experience and how it affected them before talking with them about current wars.

Senator Patrick Leahy (D-Vt.) is a strong supporter of legal abortion, partly because of an experience he had as a prosecutor when abortion was illegal. A young woman in Vermont nearly died from, and was left sterile by, a botched abortion. "Our investigation," Senator Leahy told Judge David Souter at the hearing on Souter's nomination to the Supreme Court, "found that the man arranging the abortions would bring young women from the Burlington area in Vermont, across the border to Montreal. The abortions were then performed by a woman who had learned the procedure while working for the SS at Auschwitz. The man I prosecuted would then blackmail these women after the abortion, either for money or for sex." Leahy's prosecution resulted in conviction and sent the man to prison. He suggested to Souter that the case showed "what the practical effect of outlawing abortion might be."[7]

A powerful story, but one that raises other questions Leahy may not have considered. Doesn't the fact that the Nazis were aborting their *enemies* at Auschwitz say something about abortion itself?[8] Is Leahy aware that *legal* abortionists have also botched many abortions and injured many women? Has he considered the possibility that a pregnancy aid center in Burlington—one well advertised on the University of Vermont campus there—would have given women good and life-saving alternatives to the ex-Auschwitz abortionist? Has Leahy ever talked with Feminists for Life about their program to make campuses more parent-friendly and child-friendly?[9] These are questions that Vermonters should ask the Senator.

EXPLAIN WHERE YOU'RE COMING FROM

You may not have a story as striking as Senator Leahy's; but, then again, you may. When discussion turns to eugenic abortion and someone says that "there's just no future for a child with Downs Syndrome," you may be able to say, "Hey, wait a minute! I have a little sister with Downs Syndrome. She's a happy kid and is doing pretty well in school. She's never going to be a corporate CEO or the President of the United States—but then most of us aren't, are we? Doesn't she have as much right to the pursuit of happiness as the rest of us?"

Or perhaps you majored in history in college, and you're discussing the latest war with a friend. Perhaps you can say, "You know, I was brought up in a family that always followed the flag; my ancestors and relatives fought in every American war from the Revolution to Vietnam. But in college, when I studied the Indian wars, the Mexican war, the First World War, and Vietnam, I couldn't justify our country's position. It seemed that we'd done a lot to start most of the wars we'd been involved in. That's not to say the other side was always right. Often both sides were wrong—that's how I felt about Vietnam. But that academic conclusion turned to bitter grief when my oldest brother died there. And my parents never got over it."

STRESS THE PRINCIPLES AND PEOPLE THEY ADMIRE

Politicians and others are far more likely to consider points that come from their own political or philosophical tradition than from their usual opponents. Thus, Senator Leahy might possibly listen to Feminists for Life, but he's unlikely to be impressed by someone from Pat Robertson's "700 Club." I doubt that even Feminists for Life could change Leahy's basic position on abortion; but a thoughtful and persistent approach might at least make him less vehement and activist about it.

Many liberals and radicals would just as soon pass up a chance to talk with conservative Republicans about end-of-life issues. But attorney and anti-euthanasia activist Wesley Smith has a good chance of getting to first base with them, partly because he used to work with Ralph Nader. Smith stresses class issues that matter a great deal to people on the left. He once wrote, for example, that "most leaders of the euthanasia movement, such as the author Betty Rollin and the physician Dr. Timothy Quill, are people of the 'overclass': well-off whites with a strong and supportive family or social structure who never believe they could be victimized or pressured into choosing an early death." He added that euthanasia leaders "downplay the harm that will follow for the poor, the uneducated, those without access to medical care, or the disabled, many of whom see themselves as being in the crosshairs on this issue."[10]

Not Dead Yet is a feisty group of people with disabilities who are "in the crosshairs." They organized a lively demonstration at the U.S. Supreme Court in January 1997, when the court heard two cases on doctor-assisted suicide.

In wheelchairs and on crutches, and bundled up against the cold, the demonstrators held signs that read "Endangered Species" and "We Are the Target." One of their speakers, Lucy Gwin, declared, "This is not gonna happen. We're not gonna let them do this to us." Mentioning two men who already had aided suicides, she added, "I'm mad as hell, and I'm not gonna die for Jack Kevorkian or Tim Quill. . . . We will *not* go quietly. . . . You're not gonna herd us off one at a time quietly in little rooms. We're gonna be loud about this, because we want to live!"[11] This is the kind of approach and language that people on the left can understand.

They also can understand Nat Hentoff, the outstanding civil libertarian and author who for many years has defended people with disabilities against the onslaught of eugenics and the worship of cost-effectiveness in medicine. Hentoff isn't afraid to criticize fellow journalists for sloppy and biased reporting on end-of-life issues, and he speaks out against abortion as well as euthanasia and suicide.[12]

Conservatives, too, are more likely to listen to their colleagues than to their traditional opponents. It so happens that some antiwar positions are essentially conservative. One of them, often unfairly called "isolationist," holds that the United States should refrain from meddling in the politics of other nations. It's based on a realistic view of history and the limits of power. It's also based on President George Washington's great Farewell Address, in which he warned against meddling abroad. Washington was no isolationist; he was pro-trade and favored good but arm's-length relations with other countries. "Observe good faith and justice towards all Nations," he urged. "Cultivate peace and harmony with all. . . . The Great rule of conduct for us, in regard to foreign Nations is in extending our commercial relations to have with them as little *political* connection as possible." He saw what was then our geographic isolation as a great advantage. "Why forego the advantages of so peculiar a situation?" he asked. "Why quit our own to stand upon foreign ground?"[13]

Conservatives are far more likely to listen to Washington's advice than to liberal slogans. Liberals, by the way, should also listen to Washington. Too many of them support the first stages of what seem to them grand crusades for democracy or human rights (First World War, Vietnam, Afghanistan, Iraq), only to find that those crusades themselves involve massive violations of human rights, especially the most basic of all rights—the right to life.

English writer Christopher Derrick was genuinely puzzled by the hawkishness of many conservatives. He noted that twentieth-century wars paved the way for the political left. For example, the Russian Revolution succeeded toward the end of the First World War, and the British first elected "a fully and solidly left-wing government" at the end of the Second World War. He added, "Portugal had three unwinnable Vietnams in Africa: their outcome was to radicalize—of all things—the Portuguese officer corps! And what did Vietnam itself do? It Communized Southeast Asia and radicalized a whole generation of American youth."[14]

One might add that wars immensely expand the power of government over the economy and over its citizens—power that conservatives traditionally and rightly fear. There were giant leaps in governmental power during the Civil War, the First World War, and the Second World War, as there have been in the current and open-ended war on terrorism. Wars often lead to enormous deficit spending and/or higher taxes, both of which are anathema to true conservatives.

Derrick also stressed that war "tends to destroy everything that conservatives would wish to 'conserve' at the social, cultural, moral, and religious levels. For the present cultural breakdown of the West, two World Wars are very considerably responsible." He added, "Soldiers on active service do not behave virtuously: it was an American writer, not some smug Limey, who said that the U.S. army turned the whole of South Vietnam into one vast brothel."[15] Vietnam also sent many U.S. soldiers home with terrible drug addictions and mental-health problems that contributed to family and societal breakdown in America.

On the death penalty, too, conservatives are more likely to listen to their own. "I'm opposed to the death penalty," former Nixon aide Charles Colson said. "As a political conservative, I oppose it because I don't want to give government that much power."[16] Columnist George Will, although often ambivalent about the death penalty, favorably reviewed a book that described many cases of wrongful conviction. It convinced him that "many innocent people are in prison, and some innocent people have been executed." According to Will, "Conservatives, especially, should draw this lesson from the book: Capital punishment, like the rest of the criminal justice system, is a government program, so skepticism is in order."[17] Another conservative columnist, R. Emmett Tyrrell, Jr., said that the death penalty "neither dramatizes the horror of crime nor speaks out for life. It was once thought to do both, but not in our brutal society. . . . In a society that exploits coarseness and violence in its entertainments—even in its advertisements—such niceties as retribution are lost." Speaking of a drug dealer who had committed one murder and ordered two others, Tyrrell said that he "should remain locked away for the rest of his life and unable to kill again." In prison, Tyrrell added, the man "has a chance to atone for his wrong, and by leaving him there for the right reason America has a chance to demonstrate its reverence for freedom and for life."[18]

ASK A GREAT QUESTION

Experienced lawyers know that the right question in court can turn a case in their favor. Similarly, in a dialogue on life-and-death issues, a quiet question can do much good. Generally, the goal should not be instant conversion but, rather, giving your friend something to think about.

Yet there are exceptions. Sometimes a question asked during the drama of great public debate has a major impact right away. So it was with the young John Kerry's questions to the Senate Foreign Relations Committee in 1971. A leader of Vietnam Veterans Against the War (VVAW), Kerry charged that the United States was continuing the war in Vietnam so that it wouldn't have to admit the war was a mistake. He asked the senators, "[H]ow do you ask a man to be the last man to die in Vietnam? How do you ask a man to be the last man to die for a mistake?"[19]

Many death penalty supporters say that few if any innocent people have actually been executed in the United States, at least in recent times. They may be right, although conviction overturns of people on death row (especially due to DNA evidence) make many people pause on this issue. But Reverend Lawrence Davies once framed the issue in a more personal way: "What if the one innocent person executed this year was the person you loved most dearly and deeply in all the world?"[20]

A pro-life group encouraged people to think about power issues related to abortion when it presented this quiz:

> Under current U.S. law, which is not a person?
> a) Supreme Court judge
> b) A corporation
> c) An unborn child
> Hint: Who can hire the fewest lawyers?[21]

R. Buckminster Fuller, the inventor and writer, once contemplated suicide when he faced hard times. But he asked himself, "Who am I?" He concluded, "I was an inventory of experiences. And if I did away with myself I might get rid of some connecting link of experience in the universe that would turn out to be important." He decided to stay around.[22]

But most people don't take such an intellectual approach to suicide. They are more likely to be distraught, like the young fisherman Mico Mór in Walter

Macken's great Irish novel, *Rain on the Wind.* Disappointed in love, Mico took his family's boat out to sea in a raging storm. "He was going to his death," Macken wrote, "because no man or no boat could live in a sea like this." But the violence of the storm cleared Mico's head, and he thought, "What am I doing to my poor black boat?... What am I doing at all? What will happen to my father and my mother and my grandfather if I take away their livelihood . . . ?" Those were desperate questions thrown up in a space of seconds. "And he leaned on the tiller and turned her about," bringing the boat back to shore despite the violent wind and waves.[23]

Just as a good question can start a useful train of thought, so can a good protest sign. A 2005 march against the war in Iraq included a sign featuring a picture of a mother and her three children and the ironic description, "Collateral Damage." The march took place just after Hurricane Katrina had devastated America's Gulf Coast; so a banner urged, "Make Levees, Not War," and a sign proclaimed, "National Guard Is in Wrong Gulf!" Other signs included "War *Is* Terrorism With a Bigger Budget"; "Give Peace a *Lot* of Chances"; and "Anything War Can Do Peace Can Do Better." While a bit faulty in grammar, another asked an excellent question: "Who Would Jesus Bomb?"[24]

The annual March for Life in Washington, D.C., often includes signs featuring a picture of an unborn child and the great quote from Dr. Seuss: "A person's a person, no matter how small." Other signs at the march have included "Stop the War on the Unborn"; "Abortion/Weapon of Mass Destruction"; "Keep the Dream Alive... Dreams Begin With Life"; "How Much Does an Abortion Cost? One Human Life"; and "Love Little Lives."[25]

RELATE STORIES OF THOSE WHO TURNED AROUND

It is hard to argue with combat veterans who make a case against war by describing their own experiences. Civilians tend to listen to them in respectful silence. As Veterans for Peace president David Cline has said, "[M]ost people are subjected to propaganda, and they don't really see what goes on in war... We, having experienced it, know what we are talking about." Disillusioned by the U.S. war aims when he was a soldier in Vietnam, Cline received three wounds there. In a foxhole fight, a young Vietnamese soldier shattered Cline's knee with a shot from an automatic weapon; almost simultaneously, Cline wounded the other soldier fatally. Later he looked "at this guy dead there, and I started to wonder if he had a girlfriend. I wondered how his mother was going to find out about this."[26]

There are now many veterans of the abortion wars, too, and some speak out strongly against this form of violence. They describe their difficulty in handling tiny body parts; seeing aborted babies who were born alive and struggled to keep breathing but were given no assistance; or seeing women who were badly injured by botched abortions. Some also describe terrible nightmares, long struggles with guilt, and efforts to bury guilt in alcohol and drugs. Looking back on his involvement, one ex-abortionist said he had not been "an avid abortion proponent" but, rather, "a reluctant puppet in a world gone berserk."[27]

Many governors are veterans of death penalty decisions, and some are sorry they allowed executions to go forward. The late Governor Edmund (Pat) Brown of California saved some people from the gas chamber but declined to save others. Looking back on his decisions at age eighty-three, he wrote that he had wielded "an awesome, ultimate power over the lives of others that no person or government should have, or crave." And each decision, he said, "took something out of me that nothing—not family or work or hope for the future—has ever been able to replace.[28]

Former Governor George Ryan of Illinois, originally a death penalty supporter, agonized the first time he had to decide whether to let an execution go forward. While he let the man die, he found this "the most emotional experience I have ever been through in my life," and felt that "I just couldn't do it again." Then the *Chicago Tribune* published a study describing many wrongful convictions in capital cases. Ryan, fearing that innocent people might be executed, imposed a moratorium on all Illinois executions and appointed a commission to study wrongful convictions. "If government can't get this right," he said later, "it ought not be in the business of passing such final, irreversible judgment." He finally concluded that government cannot get it right. Just before he left office in 2003, Ryan commuted the sentences of all 167 people on death row in Illinois—in most cases, to life in prison.[29]

ALTERNATIVES, ALTERNATIVES, ALTERNATIVES!

"Wouldn't you prefer a nonviolent solution to the problem, if one can be found?" This is a great question to ask about any life-and-death issue. It cuts right through rhetorical fog and gets people thinking about nonviolent solutions. You may find that your friend, despite having just made a passionate defense of some type of killing, will say, "Well, yeah, I guess so, if you can still preserve the lives and rights of the other people involved. But how can you do it?"

Then you speak of solid, workable alternatives. You describe pregnancy care centers and the Nurturing Network.[30] You explain programs of conflict resolution and civilian-based defense. You mention life in prison, with the chance and the obligation to make amends, as an alternative to the death penalty. You talk about the "Eden Alternative," which transforms nursing homes into *real* homes and thus removes fears that tempt seniors to suicide. And you outline programs that help people with severe mental illness—who often are tempted to harm themselves or others—hold jobs, hold their lives together, and have their own chance to pursue happiness.

If you can recruit old and new friends to help provide alternatives to violence, they may soon realize that there is enormous, life-affirming promise in the alternatives, but only negatives in violence. They may develop a deep commitment to nonviolence as public policy and as a way of life.

Editor's Note: While the author wrote this originally for this book, a more lengthy version appears on her Web page, www.meehanreports.com.

NOTES AND REFERENCES

1. Alvaré, Helen. March 24, 2000. Communicating the Culture of Life to a Secular Culture. Address at a conference in Washington, D.C., transcript, 3, author's files.
2. Yeats, W. B. 1956. "Easter 1916," in his *The Collected Poems of W. B. Yeats*. New York: Macmillan, pp. 177–180. Quote from p. 179.
3. Burns, Stewart. 2004. *To the Mountaintop*. New York: HarperCollins, p. 15.
4. McCorvey, Norma and Gary Thomas. 1997. *Won by Love*. Nashville, TN: Thomas Nelson.
5. Meehan, Mary. Spring/Summer, 2000. The Ex-abortionists: Why They Quit. *Human Life Review, 26*(2/3), 7–28, 8 and 21. A slightly different version of the article appears on http://www.meehanreports.com.
6. Prejean, Helen. 1993. *Dead Man Walking*. New York: Random House, pp. 109, 118–119, 131–140, 166–168, 223–241. Quote from p. 229.
7. U.S. Senate, Committee on the Judiciary. September 1990. Hearing on *Nomination of David H. Souter to Be Associate Justice of the Supreme Court of the United States*, 101st Cong., 2nd sess., p. 270.
8. See Perry, Mike W. July, 1988. The Sound of the Machine. *The Freeman 38*, (7), pp. 257–262, on the Nazis and abortion.
9. Callahan, Nicole M. Summer/Fall 2004. Revolution on Campus and Seeds of Change at Georgetown. *American Feminist*, 3–14; and http://www.feministsforlife.org.

10. Smith, Wesley J. 1997. *Forced Exit.* New York: Times Books/Random House, pp. 9–10.
11. Quoted in Meehan, Mary. January 19–25, 1997. Handicapped to Court: "We Want to Live." *National Catholic Register,* 1 and 11.
12. See Nat Hentoff's 1983–1984 series of *Village Voice* articles on Baby Doe cases, reprinted in *Human Life Review, 10*(2) (Spring 1984), 73–104; his "You Don't Have to Believe in God to Be Prolife," *U.S. Catholic,* March 1989, 28–30; and his November–December 2003 *Village Voice* articles on Terri Schiavo, reprinted in *Human Life Review, 29*(4) (Fall 2003), 80–89.
13. George Washington, "Farewell Address," September 19, 1796, in John C. Fitzpatrick, ed., *The Writings of George Washington* (Washington, D.C.: U.S. Government Printing Office, 1931–1944), vol. 35, pp. 231, 233, and 234. (In the first sentence quoted, I have spelled out the abbreviated "towds.")
14. Derrick, Christopher. September 1981. Bombs and Babies: Three Baffling Questions. *New Oxford Review,* pp. 2–3.
15. Ibid.
16. Colson, Charles W. October 27, 1982. "Prisons Are Leper Colonies in America," interview with *USA Today,* p. 9-A.
17. Will, George F. April 6, 2000. Innocent on Death Row. *Washington Post,* p. A-23. He was reviewing Barry Scheck and others, *Actual Innocence* (2000). New York: Doubleday/Random House.
18. Tyrrell, R. Emmett. December 12, 2000. Death Penalty Interregnum. *Washington Times,* p. A-21.
19. U.S. Senate, Committee on Foreign Relations. April–May 1971. Hearing on *Legislative Proposals Relating to the War in Southeast Asia,* 92nd Cong., 1st sess., p. 183.
20. Davies, Lawrence A. September 1982. Unto the Least of These. *theOtherSide,* pp. 15–16.
21. "Equal Rights: Or How Society Protects Almost Each and Every Person" (Minneapolis, MN: SOUL, n.d.), p. 12.
22. Quoted in Weil, Martin. July 3, 1983. R. Buckminster Fuller Dies at 87 of Heart Attack. *Washington Post,* p. B-6.
23. Macken, Walter. 1950. *Rain on the Wind.* New York: Macmillan, pp. 304–312.
24. Photographs of September 24, 2005, antiwar march, Washington, D.C., by the author.
25. Photographs of March for Life, Washington, D.C., in January of 1988, 1992, 2003, and 2005, by the author. The Dr. Seuss quote is from Theodor Seuss Geisel (1954). *Horton Hears a Who!* New York: Random House.
26. Cline, David. September 2004. "A Responsibility to My People," interview by Daniel Redwood, posted on htttp://www.veteransforpeace.org (see "VFP In the News"). September 17, 2002.
27. Hill, McArthur. Quoted in Meehan, The Ex-abortionists, p. 18.

28. Edmund (Pat), Brown and Dick Adler. 1989. *Public Justice, Private Mercy*. New York: Weidenfeld & Nicolson, p. 163.

29. Shapiro, Bruce. January 8 and 15, 2001. A Talk with Governor George Ryan. *The Nation*, p. 17; Lydersen, Kari. March, 2002. Death Penalty Foes See Progress in Ill. *Washington Post*, p. A-2; Pierre, Robert E. and Kari Lydersen. January 12, 2003. Illinois Death Row Emptied. *Washington Post*, pp. A-1 and A-11; and Hockstader, Lee. January 17, 2003. Off Ill. Death Row, to a Rougher Place, *Washington Post*, p. A-3.

30. Phone numbers for the largest U.S. ones are: Birthright, 1-800-550-4900; Care Net 1-800-395-HELP (800-395-4357); Heartbeat International 800-395-HELP (1-800-395-4357); National Life Center 800-848-LOVE (1-800-848-5683); Nurturing Network 800-TNN-4MOM (1-800-866-4666).

The Law's Role in the Consistent Life Ethic

Carol Crossed

"The law cannot make you love me. But it can keep you from lynching me."[1]

—*Dr. Martin Luther King, Jr.*

Here is a common parable with some embellishments.

There once was a village and a river ran through its center. Each day at 4:00, the church bells chimed and villagers went to pray for people who were drowning in the river. Farmers put down ploughs, students put aside books, and mothers took children by the hand and walked to the church to plead to the Almighty to save the people.

This went on for years, until a wise woman passed through. She marveled at the faith of the people. But she had a better idea: Why not go to the banks of the river and pull out those in the water, throw out inner tubes, or teach swimming lessons?

And so every day at 4:00 when the church bells rang, some went into the church to pray and others went to the water and pulled out the drowning people. Some taught swimming lessons; others raised money to buy inner tubes and life preservers.

This went on for years, until a wise peddler passed through. The sage was in awe of the faithfulness of the townspeople who loved their neighbors so much. But an idea occurred: Besides praying and offering charity, why not go upstream and find out why people were falling in the water and what they could do to prevent it?

Now, many were unsure they wanted to do this and feared the answer they might find on the bridge. Could it be the villagers ran across the bridge with such reckless abandon that they pushed off those in their way?

The poor were in their way because they demanded tax money for health care. Women and their unborn are disposable because unwanted children will overpopulate the world. In their rush to get to the other side, they pushed off the bridge those on death row, who threaten our civil society with costly appeals. Bombing is the solution to global neighbors who may harbor weapons of mass destruction that threaten our existence.

Prayer isolated some from ever seeing the problem. And charity at the edge is neat and measurable. We see the tears we wipe away as we work in soup kitchens and crisis pregnancy centers. We use warm towels to dry those we pull out of the river, and see the smiles of the homeless and the drug-addicted.

But how do we prevent people from going overboard? We hold signs to try to change people's hearts from running. We educate through workshops and conferences about others on the bridge who are weaker. We hold rallies and processions to get everyone's attention. Some even sit nonviolently across the bridge to block the way of those who are running.

But while we pray in our churches, do charitable works at the river's edge, raise awareness, and work for justice for the less powerful, they are still being destroyed. While we delve into why there are abortions, executions, poverty and war—the unborn, the elderly, and victims of war are still falling into the water.

What can we do? We petition the government to play a role in protecting people by building side rails on the bridge. This act of preventing harm with the assistance of the government is the dimension of law.

THE RELATIONSHIP OF JUSTICE AND PEACE TO THE LAW

If you are like most people, one of these responses to helping particularly resonates with you. For me, it is nonviolent civil disobedience—sitting on the bridge, blocking people's path, calling attention to the "Slow down" sign. No major social injustice has ever been solved without people willing to break the law: Apartheid, women's suffrage, ethnic cleansing, denial of rights for racial minorities, child labor practices, and human rights violations in dictatorships.

The one particularly close to my heart is the attempted protection of the American Indian. My great-grandmother was Mary Risen, a Cherokee from the Eastern Band. Only forty years before her birth, in The Trail of Tears, her people were forcibly removed from the southeastern United States to

Oklahoma. The Moravians, a religious sect from Germany, sat on their land in Georgia to try to prevent their forced removal to Oklahoma. After all, the American Indians were human beings who deserved rights.

Like most of the workers on the bridge, one does not experience success immediately, or maybe not in one's lifetime, or maybe not at all. The work of peace and justice is abstract, immeasurable, invisible victories. And it is often anonymous. A vigil for a death row inmate is for all the prisoners on death row. A sit-in at an abortion clinic is on behalf of all women contemplating aborting their child; a rally against any war supports all military personnel and the countless thousands of enemies they will destroy.

During the anti-Vietnam War movement, a popular slogan was "What if there was a war and no one came?" What if we were so successful with education and raising consciousness that no guardrails would need to be built? It would not matter if the death penalty were legal because no warden would pull the switch. What if people's hearts were so won over that nobody showed up at the army recruitment office? What if a construction worker could not be found to install plumbing at an abortion clinic? Stories abound of courageous people refusing to participate in violence in these ways. This is the personalism of Dorothy Day and the Catholic Worker Movement today.

After an arrest, someone will invariably ask me, "Why do you break the law? Why do you not just change the law?" In other words, why not build guardrails on the bridge?

The answer is not either one or the other, but both the strategies are needed. Civil disobedience is a strategy that may change people's hearts over time, but building guardrails is critical to prevent people from dying now. It is sophistry to believe that the thousands dying in Iraq are less important than changing the hearts of their aggressors in the future; that the thousands of babies being destroyed this year at a clinic are less important than creating a world of economic safety nets in place next year for their mothers; and that the hundreds of disabled and elderly being euthanized are less important than establishing a culture that down the line will cherish our aged.

Every second Friday in Rochester, New York, a vigil is sponsored by The Reconciliation Network, an anticapital punishment group. Passersby angrily ask us what we are doing about crime on the streets to make the death penalty unnecessary. My response? I am not sure I am doing anything. While others focus on reducing the city's homicide rate, I want to change our state's death penalty law that takes the life of the killer.

Accusations about doing something about injustice are also prevalent at sites where abortions are performed. One hears, "Don't change the law to make abortion illegal. Help to make abortion unnecessary." Go down to the edge of the water and pull out those women who have been raped, have violent partners, or cannot afford day care. Go up on the bridge to increase social services so that low-income families have affordable housing and single mothers have education subsidies.

Like reducing the need for the death penalty, reducing the need for abortion is necessary.

But what some members of the pro-life movement may be saying is that while we are creating a society that values mothers and the unborn, let us build guardrails to protect them from abortion in the meantime. Which is better is not the issue. It is a question of how a community can do both.

The nonviolent strategies to protect the unprotected should be viewed as equally important. Prayer services and acts of charity nurture the soul and body. All components of justice and peace on the bridge are indispensable strategies and valued equally. Those who commit civil disobedience, who educate, who protest, and who legislate, all contribute to keeping everyone on the bridge.

PHILOSOPHIES OF GOVERNING THAT LIMIT THE LAW

Some nondemocratic forms of government do not concern themselves with the interaction of individuals and their responsibilities toward one another. Totalitarianism does not care if people fall off the bridge. Rather, the individual is a commodity used to further nationalistic pursuits and is pushed overboard afterward. Here we will explore the use of law by democratic or representative governments, which represent the approval of the majority of their citizens.

Some philosophical persuasions within democracies disagree that the government has a role in protecting people from harm or disagree on the extent of the government's role in it.

Anarchy sees the government's predominant role as protecting the rights of individual citizens from being limited or restricted—the best government is less government. Immanuel Kant articulates this principle by instructing citizens to act in such a way that the liberty of one's will can coexist with the liberty of the will of others. To the pure anarchist, a person who steals does not violate the principle as long as he or she does not ask the state to deny the same liberty to fellow citizens.

Forms of modified anarchy are libertarianism and personalism. Libertarianism is best understood in the economic realm as a laissez-faire doctrine disallowing government's interference in capitalism. This egalitarian principle at first seems magnanimous. If a government would interfere with capitalist enterprise to establish a minimum wage, then an industrial magnate who pays substandard wages is not infringing upon anyone else's freedom, because the libertarian concedes that liberty to everyone else.

The "universal law" Kant defines is not a civil or moral law but the universal law of liberty. Every person's understanding of freedom is relative. There is no objective truth upon which liberty hinges. This in effect encourages the creation of a society of the intelligentsia over the slow-witted; the powerful over the weak; the cunning over the innocent; the wealthy over the poor.

Personalism is the operative principle of the Catholic Worker Movement. It is akin to anarchy in that government is seen as a superfluous player amid the rights and freedom of the individual. But the similarities stop there. The government is not relied upon to establish guardrails, but the individuals' personal moral codes demand that they themselves address human suffering. This way of life is alive in countless communities throughout the United States. Individuals take the place of government in the duty to protect the weak from harm. They practice personally the role of the government in their socialistic concern for the poor, the aborted, and the person on death row, to the extent of giving up the individualistic emphasis on the rights that anarchists see as central.[2]

The degree to which Catholic Worker Movements oppose legislation is evolving and appears contradictory. In the 1960s, many Worker Houses remained true to personalism and did not support the civil rights legislation. Instead, they supported civil disobedience to advance the rights of the Negro. Today, some communities may not support legislation to stop abortion. But many communities like the Los Angeles Catholic Worker support civil disobedience in front of abortion clinics. Most would support social programs for the poor. Others support legislation to curb militarism or racism.

What all of these forms of political structures have in common is the "nonrole" government plays in protecting the dignity of every person.

MORALITY AND LAW

> *"On [President Eisenhower's] way out of a church service in which he heard a sermon on the need for new civil rights laws, Ike shook hands with the Navy chaplain and said, 'You can't legislate morality.' "*[3]

How often does one hear "You can't legislate morality?" This quote was made popular during the Civil Rights Movement, with an attempt to prevent the force of law from being imposed on the public and private moralities behind segregation.

A common definition of morality speaks of civil behavior held in common about what is right and wrong. This assumes an objective dimension to morality: that certain behaviors can be commonly considered right and others wrong. It also assumes social and cultural dimensions that have collective agreement.

Today, the social dimension of racism is not defended. Few among us argue whether discrimination against ethnic groups constitutes immoral behavior that should involve the law, a viewpoint the segregationists in King's time refused to accept. This social dimension of morality is critical to any discussion about the consistent life ethic and law.

Not all or even most private behaviors effecting civil relationships are legislated. It is more socially acceptable to say "Please" and "Thank you," certainly legal not to do so. However, a private store owner's refusal to hire people due to race is moral private behavior that infringes on another person's human right.

Segregationists attempted to reduce a social evil to private or personal moral behavior. The tension around consistent life ethic issues, particularly abortion and euthanasia, has roots in this obfuscation of what is private and what is social.

RELIGION AND LAW

Because of the close association of religion and morality, they are often used interchangeably when talking about law. "You can't legislate morality" is often interpreted to mean "politics and religion don't go together," otherwise known as "the separation of church and state."

A separation between the two has evolved in most democracies, but in some, civil law and religion do share a commonality under the law. Some enforce a particular dress; taxes raised in some countries pay for the upkeep of houses of worship.

Today, in democracies that honor the separation, religious laws still exist. But they are laws not held in common. Whether one goes to mass on Sunday or eats kosher foods is not in the purview of democracies to enforce because these are ecclesiastical laws governing personal moral codes. They do not involve the common good or the protection of another person.

If there is one universal law that prevails on the bridge and is common to most religions, it is the ethic of reciprocity:

Hinduism: "Do naught unto others which would cause you pain if done unto you."

Judaism: "What is hateful to you, do not to your fellow man. This is the law."

Christianity: "In everything, do unto others as you would like them to do unto you."
Humanism: "Don't do things you wouldn't want to have done to you."

This ethic is where morality and religion overlap and is the basis for law. The fight against segregation was preached in Baptist churches in the South and discussed in synagogues in the East. Civil rights leader Dr. Martin Luther King, Jr. was a Christian minister; God was invoked before every rally. Scripture verses were quoted and gospel music predominated at prayer services for integration.

But segregation was a universal human rights issue religious people felt compelled to address. They were not compelling people to attend Sunday church service or tithe to their temple. Their private morality saw segregation as a sin against God, and therefore private acts to eradicate it were seen as virtue.

But establishing laws that protected the rights of the Negro went beyond private morality because it involved the protection of another person. It was a social morality more universal than the laws of Christianity or Judaism. Segregation was a violation of the natural law that people of faith, or people of no faith, felt compelled to oppose.

Creating guardrails that advance human rights has historically had religious people as a significant component: Evangelical Christians were central to the abolition of slavery. Quakers were at the forefront of women's suffrage. Roman Catholics led the anti-Vietnam War movement. The private morality of these religious groups compelled them to advocate the enforcement by government of a social morality they believed all people, religious or not, could understand.

A distinction can be made: Religion and belief in an afterlife may make the strongest case for believers to *act* upon correcting a wrong. But religion is only one of several persuasions to make the case for *why* a certain behavior is wrong. Religion is a subset of the broader questions surrounding what is moral. Morality may have a religious component but is not religion itself.

Since the antisegregationists of the 1950s and 1960s, our awareness about world religions has increased dramatically. Greater communication and mobility have expanded not only our knowledge of other faiths, but also a greater appreciation for the rights of others to hold differing religious beliefs. Hence, believers in Christianity are challenged by believers in the Jewish tradition. Believers in the Hindu faith are challenged by believers in the tenets of Buddhism.

The presence of diversity demands a more complex response to social problems and application of law. A global awareness of the different perspectives of who God is and what God demands from God's followers creates a dilemma for lawmakers. Because the majority of democracies are composed of diverse belief systems, the morality or immorality of certain behaviors is less universally defined. The body politic increasingly experiences tension about how to judge behaviors

Do not push another off the bridge if you yourself do not want to be pushed. The simplicity of this offers clarity, but only to a point. Cultures whose various religions demand they love their neighbor as they love themselves are irreconcilably challenged by the ever-evolving and ever-devolving bodies of religious thought. How does one interpret who is one's neighbor? How does one choose to be treated oneself? How does one extend that concern to others? How far should one be compelled to extend that concern?

Without a common determination of how actions affect for the better or worse the greater good, modifications in moral conduct may be less likely to occur, or may not even occur at all. Religion should never cease to amplify answers about how to treat others as one wants to be treated. But this universal question about law and morality can no longer be left in its entirety to religion alone.

The accusation that a particular morality is the expression of religion or one particular religion serves to obfuscate the public dialogue about guardrails.

Add to this the body of thought that does not believe in a higher power directing our behavior or to whom we are responsible. Are atheists exempted from universal truths? Or can atheists lend an understanding to developing these truths?

What is at stake is who will live and who will die. As much as the atomic bomb forever changed questions about war and peace, abortion has forever changed the meaning of human life and our responsibility to it. Wars rage and often do so even in the name of religion. Civil and global strife directly deprive millions of their very lives. Killing in the name of personal or national security occurs through capital punishment, abortion, and endless incidences of torture.

For too long, the discussion of these questions has been relegated to religious argumentation. For too long there has been too little attempt to find a common denominator for understanding their relationship. For too long there have been bodies of fragmented thought that pit the rights of one over the rights of the other.

Religious persuasiveness must not be abandoned, replaced, or deleted. But if that argumentation can be enhanced legitimately with sound secular and scientific principles, it will be more universally accepted.

For instance, the onset of human life is not a dogma of religion but a fact of science. The humanity of the unborn does not have to be found in the Bible or Qu'ran. It can be found in a college textbook on embryology.

The firepower of nuclear armaments and their capacity to destroy all living things does not have to be found through prayer with our Creator. It can be found on any Web site that carries military science journals.

How much more convenient the ethic of reciprocity would be if we needed to rely on religion instead of the perils of human genetic engineering or military science. In Galileo's era, religion was criticized for not recognizing scientific information. Today, can religion be criticized when it insists on and demands societal recognition of science?

That will then allow the convictions of the religious and humanist alike to act upon a course of moral conduct to legislate the protection of the vulnerable.

LEGISLATING "CHOICE" WITHOUT COMMUNITY

> *"If you don't like irradiated food then don't eat it."*
>
> *—An automobile bumper sticker spotted in New York*

Despite the fact that laws *prohibiting* euthanasia have protected the dying and the disabled in the past, laws *allowing* it appear to be on the increase. This is not the trend in most countries regarding the death penalty. Few countries allow capital punishment. But even in the United States, recent laws have narrowed its use. To better determine guilt or innocence of someone on death row, a law was established in 2003 to permit the use of DNA testing when appropriate before an execution. And in 2005, the U.S. Supreme Court placed a ban on executions of persons who were under the age of eighteen when the crime was committed.

Encouraging governments to build guardrails to protect unborn children and their mothers has been more difficult. If protecting children before birth is a human right,[4] why do no laws prohibit abortion or severely restrict it in the United States? This would bring it more in alignment with most other countries that only allow abortion at or before twelve weeks of in-utero age.

A friend who had an abortion twenty-five years ago is undergoing the journey of postabortion healing from psychological and emotional pain. Although she says legislating against abortion will make little difference, she admitted that she probably would not have had her own abortion if it were illegal. Why? Because, she said, deep inside she knew it was morally wrong. If a law had been in place to protect her, it would have confirmed her innate conviction that killing was wrong.

If abortion takes a human life, why should it not be against the law? Is there something instructive about what is in the law? Could it be that law is a teacher, as it would have been for my friend? When the U.S. Supreme Court case *Brown v. Board of Education* desegregated schools in the 1950s, were people in the South ready for it? Apparently not, since rage, looting, and arrests multiplied in the 1960s. Today it hardly seems possible to imagine the strides toward integration we have made. While it does not seem that people changed the law, over the fifty years of its existence, it does seem that the law has changed people. The very existence of guardrails was a tutorial on why they were built.

In contrast, *Roe v. Wade*, decided in 1973, took down the guardrails. After more than thirty years, it contributed nothing to advancing acceptability of abortion as a moral good or even as a moral neutrality. Some would argue that unlike other longstanding moral issues like women's rights, time has actually increased its unacceptability.

Others say abortion is a "personal" decision and therefore not a political issue. It is in fact a personal decision like joining the military or choosing to be euthanized. But like other consistent life ethic issues, it is a personal decision that affects someone other than one's self, and therefore is a social issue. A vulnerable person is going overboard, therefore justifying the need for establishing guardrails.

In the final analysis, "choice" sets back the progress of the consistent life ethic because it undermines the social character of the taking of another's life.

A STRATEGY OF CONNECTEDNESS

The consistent life ethic calls us to more than a philosophical discussion. It is also a strategy. In addition to deciding that all vulnerable people deserve legal protection, it is a challenge to do so effectively.

People on the bridge work to find the answers to *why*: Why are people poor? Why are unborn children and their mothers rejected? Why is there crime that creates the kind of insecurity that demands the death penalty? Why are there dictatorships that oppress people? While we seek justice for the poor, the unborn, the death row inmate, and the victims of war, we establish human guardrails, the laws in a representative government that prevent people from being pushed overboard. The work of peace does not allow for thousands to die while the work of justice is going on.

Those who protect the death row inmate stand on the bridge's side. Those who fight the injustice of war stand on the bridge's side. Those who protect the sick and the unborn stand on the bridge's side.

But what happens if we stand like totem poles, staunch and straight, our arms to our side, refusing to reach out to the other person next to us? The person defending the death row inmate needs to stretch to reach the hand of the person defending the unborn. Antiwar activists need to stretch to hold hands with the person protecting the disabled and the elderly.

There can be no holes in the chain which allow the vulnerable to slip through between our staunch erect bodies. Instead, we stretch. We reach. We touch. We bend. We give up being territorial and acknowledge that the person we are protecting is as important as the persons others next to us are protecting. We refuse to be fragmented by polarizing political ideologies that say the laws I am establishing are more important than the laws you are establishing. We allow our space on the bridge to be shared with those who have a vision that complements our own. Only this way will the guardrail on the bridge be a human continuum and all human life be protected.

NOTES AND REFERENCES

1. Notables and Quotables, *Wall Street Journal,* November 13, 1962, p. 18.
2. Rourke, Thomas and Rosita Chazarreata Rourke. 2005. *Theory of Personalism.* New York: Lexington Books.
3. Branch, Taylor. 1988. *Parting the Waters: America in the King Years 1954–63.* New York: Simon and Schuster, p. 213.
4. Proclaimed by *General Assembly Resolution 1386(XIV)* of November 20, 1959, third paragraph of the Preamble.

Pro-life Politics: From Counter-Movement to Transforming Movement

James R. Kelly

James R. Kelly is a professor of sociology at Fordham University. These excerpts come from a keynote speech at the 2001 Conference of the University Faculty for Life, with some of the extensive endnotes woven into the text and edited for conciseness.

We should have no trouble understanding why right-to-life pioneers chose to be "single issue," linking abortion only with infanticide and euthanasia. They came from all walks of life, many faith traditions, were political novices—practically apolitical—and could agree quickly that abortion killed a developing human life and thus, could never be a moral choice and should not be legal. The main recruitment tactic was not church teachings but pictures of fetal development or aborted fetuses. Dr. Jack Willke, president of the National Right to Life Committee during the 1980s, credits the massive distribution of these graphic photos for pre-*Roe* defeats of the 1972 Michigan and South Dakota referenda to legalize abortion. Activists found it telling that supporters of legal abortion agreed to debate them publicly only after they promised not to exhibit pictures.

The first abortion opponents were not purely single issue, since the movement presciently predicted the reemergence of the euthanasia movement and dangers legal abortion posed for those handicapped and retarded. So there was not merely a counterreaction to legal abortion activism but anticipation of other threats. Still, the term *counter* before "movement" applied; right-to-life pioneers talked about *restoring* the right to life mostly by *opposing* and *defeating* those promoting legal abortion.

Nevertheless, the first truly national right-to-life grassroots organization were in the "service wing." These groups realized the inadequacy of opposing abortion without helping unwillingly pregnant women or those who could not afford to be pregnant. In 1970, Louise Somerhill founded Birthright to provide counseling, financial assistance, medical help, and private "birthright" homes for women whose futures were threatened by an unwanted pregnancy. In 1971, Lori Maier founded Alternatives to Abortion International. Since then many groups have started similar services—more than 3,000 such centers are in the United States alone. There are now far more such centers in the U.S. than abortion clinics. While impressive, these groups are charities rather than justice-seeking groups. They aim at helping women choose birth rather than changing structures for women's equality and a culture of life.

But initially there was little in antiabortion movement discourse that explicitly promoted any *transformation* of culture and social life to produce the new structures or consciousness to augment human dignity comprehensively. Indeed, the growth in the movement's political sophistication in the United States mostly led to connections with the Republican Party that historical analysis shows impeded talk of transformation. In the technical vocabulary of social movement scholars, during the 1980s and 1990s the movement tactically expanded its "resource capacity" and achieved some influence on the Republican Party leadership—at the cost of depleting its strategic "hearts and minds" capacities. The movement's public identification with fiscal conservatives opposing programs aiding working and middle class families made it less likely that "bystanders" would associate opposition to abortion with economic or social justice.

Ironically, the movement's initial post-*Roe* political hopes resided largely with the Democratic Party which, at that time, was the party identification of the majority of activists, who were disproportionately Roman Catholic. Ellen McCormack was the housewife leader of the Long Island "Women for the Unborn" and later a founder of the Right-to-Life Party. Her quixotic 1975 campaign for president in twenty Democratic state primaries was the U.S. movement's first explicitly political action. While McCormack's 1975 tactic was unanimously supported, her 1979 second run was almost universally criticized. By 1979, Ronald Reagan was a candidate for president, and he promised abortion opponents he would work to reverse *Roe*. For the next quarter-century the Republican Party was identified as the political home for abortion opponents and the Democrats for committed pro-choice activists. Only after the 2004 elections, with two straight Democratic presidential losses and over a decade of being the minority congressional party, did the national Democratic leadership begin, ever so hesitantly, to allow that its national candidates might present their position on abortion as nuanced. Before, it had been absolutist, the complete equivalent of a morally unquestioned civil right troublesome only to bigots or the unenlightened.

While abortion opponents readily acknowledge that things did not turn out to be what Reagan had promised, they mistakenly blame only extrinsic factors and overlook the intrinsic limitations of the Reagan administration's pro-life commitments. If the movement does not grasp why a Reagan-led Republican Party could not undo legal abortion, it will make the movement permanently vulnerable to a corrosive nostalgia which will lead to discouragement, thwarting maturation from *counter* to *transformative*.

THE LIMITED AND LIMITING REAGAN PRO-LIFE EMBRACE

Activists quickly noticed that Reagan put abortion on the "back burner" to pursue tax reductions and increased military spending. In her 1996 critical "insider's" account of this period, Tanya Melich[1] reports that most of the delegates viewed Reagan's courting of antiabortion activists as a shrewd tactic to add numbers to a declining party base, which had slid to 20 percent of the total voters. The 1976 Republican Convention delegate vote on including the anti-*Roe* constitutional amendment in the Party Platform was scheduled after midnight, with debate limited to four speakers. Melich is certain that pro-choice delegates had enough states ready to call for a roll-call vote on including a constitutional amendment overturning *Roe*. But they were ignored by the Convention Chairman, John Rhodes, who called for a voice vote. Without certainty, Rhodes declared that a majority had voted anti-*Roe*. Melich doubts if most delegates supported the constitutional amendment. Beyond doubt is that polls of delegates routinely show that the majority does not support the call for a constitutional amendment overturning *Roe*. Almost all studies of donors to both parties, but especially to the Republican Party, show they are overwhelmingly *fiscal* conservatives and *social liberals*. Just as they affirm values of *free* trade and consumer *choice*, so too *free choice* in matters of "personal" morality.

While the party's tactical opening up to abortion opponents benefited it by adding many working and lower-middle-class moral traditionalists to its voting base, it is much less certain that it strategically helped the pro-life cause. Even Melich acknowledges that "[t]he religious right played a major role in electing the new Republican majority, not only in delivering votes but in grassroots organizing and raising campaign contributions."[2] She estimates that the

"Christian Right" alone mobilized 4 million activists who reached 50 million voters. As an "insider," Melich sounds shrewd when saying that because most Republicans want this grassroots support without alienating their pro-choice majority, the core Republican leadership kept an astute silence about abortion. They followed the June 1984 campaign advice of one of Reagan's inner circle, Bob Teeter, that "It's one issue we ought not to talk about. . . They (abortion opponents) know where we stand, and we've got a lot of people on the other side."[3]

Another insider, Douglas W. Kmiec, who directed the Office of Legal Counsel during the first Reagan administration, perceptively pointed out that in each of the Reagan administration's challenges to *Roe*, the Justice Department never explicitly endorsed any of the three core right-to-life contentions: a developing human life possesses a right to life starting at conception, abortion kills a human person, or that abortion should be illegal.[4] To be sure, the solicitor generals did contest both *Roe's* extension of the privacy doctrine to abortion and the Court's striking down (until the 1989 *Webster* ruling) of any state's legislative efforts to protect the unborn after viability; but, he notes, these briefs never directly challenged the core pro-choice position that abortion should be legal. Kmiec tried but could not persuade the Reagan Justice Department to use language that did explicitly reflect the core right-to-life issue: that abortion killed not a "potential" but a developing human life. When he reviewed the administration briefs, Kmiec persistently sought to substitute terms reflecting Reagan's public and explicit endorsement of this. Where the briefs used the *Roe* Court's phrase "potential life," Kmiec tried to substitute "prenatal life." Each time, his revision was ignored. Kmiec's language changes, if adopted, could have prepared for a foundational critique of *Roe*, as opposed to the post-Webster deferential to *Roe* "right to know" abortion facts and available abortion alternatives in the 1992 *Casey* decision at the end of the Reagan–Bush era. Kmiec ruefully recalls that his efforts to raise the core right-to-life principle resulted only in finding himself "out of the loop."

At the end of his careful and sympathetic review of right-to-life "victories" during the Reagan administration, Donald T. Critchlow concludes that "[i]n the end, economics within the Reagan administration had won over the social issues."[5] To grasp the political improbability fiscal conservatives would support pro-life policies that impede market efficiency, it is important to realize that the right-to-life experience with their Republican tactical allies fits the larger pattern Francome found in his worldwide comparative study of abortion law changes.[6] After a short period of opposing legal abortion, fiscal conservatives and their political parties everywhere come to support legal abortion to control births of what they take to be the "unproductive" classes.

Put another way, we can expect Reagan's fiscal-social conservatism will, under pressures of this internal tension, continue to politically morph into the *fiscal conservative-social liberal* Republicanism of, say, Christie Whitman, Pete Wilson, William Weld, and Republican elites. As for Reagan's immediate successors, George H.W. Bush and Robert Dole, Robert G. Morrison did a scathing review of their sheer tactical arrangement with right-to-life leaders. He concludes,

> Pro-lifers have pursued a "pragmatist" strategy of endorsing whichever Republican seems likely to win, providing that his record is, or can be made to seem even modestly pro-life. We have clamored for "our place at the table," with less attention to what is being served... This has been offered as the responsible thing to do. After all, millions of lives are at stake.
>
> But these unconvinced "pro-life champions" are ultimately not very convincing. On the one question in public life where the American people can smell insincerity, these men exude insincerity. And, in retirement... Ford, Bush, and Dole have used their positions as party elders against pro-lifers. That alone should give us pause. Are we to continue to back whichever compromised and compromising figure the establishment offers up?[7]

Reagan Supreme Court appointees Sandra Day O'Connor and Anthony Kennedy (with Bush appointee David Souter) comprised the core of the 1992 *Casey* decision that rooted *Roe* in the Court's need for a "legitimacy" that reversal would weaken. This shows again the cogency of Francome's observation that fiscal conservatives are quickly won over to a pro-choice position (except for government funding of abortion). Francesco Alberoni astutely observed all authentic social movements, because they promote greater solidarity, are implicitly anti-capitalist.[8] As the movement claims abortion is not what most women want but choose when they run out of choices, then the tactical alignment of right-to-life moral conservatives with free-market fiscal conservatives must inevitably be experienced as strategically distorting.

Critchlow provides another summary which serves as a segue to my main theme: How might the *right-to-life* movement become *pro-life?* How can a movement classified as a reactionary counter-movement become recognized as a transformative movement whose core is progressive, egalitarian, and nonviolent? Critchlow concludes that at the end of the twentieth century, antiabortion activists felt pessimistic. "From their perspective, the political fight had gone against them. They viewed recent Supreme Court decisions as victories for the abortion movement. In the end, the Supreme Court had not overturned *Roe*... anti-abortionists had been ostracized by the Democratic party; and the Republican party appeared divided on the issue, and talk of the 'gender gap' portended a reversal of the party's antiabortion position. State legislation to restrict the number of abortions had been overturned to all extents and purposes by activist judges. The media seemed hostile, portraying anti-abortionists as fanatics and members of the Christian Right as bigoted extremists."[9]

THE EMERGENCE OF THE CONSISTENT ETHIC OF LIFE AS A CRYSTALLIZING TERM

On December 6, 1983, the late Joseph Cardinal Bernardin gave the annual Gannon Lecture at Fordham University and retrieved from the movement's collective memory one of the few fresh phrases in the stale two-decade-old debate. He entitled his address "A Consistent Ethic of Life: An American Catholic Dialogue."[10] Bernardin was invited to speak on the American Bishops' just-published and widely noted pastoral letter on the morality of nuclear weapons, *The Challenge to Peace*. His audience and reporters present expected a discussion of the letter's moral critiques of the Reagan administration's expansionist military policies and the doctrine of Mutually Assured Destruction. But Bernardin surprised everybody by announcing he would talk about abortion—but in the larger context of the Church's evolving teaching about war and peace.

Though uncommon, Bernardin's conjoining of war and the abortion should not have surprised literate and attached Catholics. Seven months before, the Bishops taught in their pastoral letter that the same moral principle governed both the classical just war principle of "discrimination" (prohibiting any direct targeting of noncombatants) and the traditional prohibition against direct induced abortion: "Nothing can justify the direct attack on innocent human life, in or out of warfare. Abortion is precisely such an attack."[11]

The Bishops acknowledged that many who opposed nuclear weapons did not also oppose abortion. They said, "We must ask how long a nation willing to extend a constitutional guarantee to the 'right' to kill defenseless human beings by abortion is likely to refrain from adopting strategic warfare policies deliberately designed to kill millions of defenseless human beings, if adopting them should come to seem 'expedient.'" Bernardin hoped for a dialogue on all the life issues and invited abortion opponents and supporters to dialogue under the shared framework of consistency.

> If one contends, as we do, that the right of every fetus to be born should be protected by civil law and supported by civil consensus, then our moral, political and economic responsibilities do not stop at the moment of birth. Those who defend the right to life of the weakest among us must be equally visible in support of the quality of life of the powerless among us: the old and the young, the hungry and the homeless, the undocumented immigrant and the unemployed worker. Such a quality of life posture translates into specific political and economic positions on tax policy, employment generation, welfare policy, nutrition and feeding programs, and health care. Consistency means we cannot have it both ways. We cannot urge a compassionate society and vigorous public policy to protect the rights of the unborn and then argue that compassion and significant public programs on behalf of the needy undermine the moral fiber of the society or are beyond the proper scope of governmental responsibility.

Bernardin added that while "the spectrum of life cuts across the issues of genetics, abortion, capital punishment, modern warfare, and the care of the terminally ill . . . these are all distinct problems, enormously complicated, and deserving individual treatment. No single answer and no simple responses will solve them."

Moreover, he noted at present "No other major institution presently holds these two positions (linking abortion and war) in the way the Catholic Bishops now do." He also acknowledged that while "A consistent ethic of life must be held by a constituency to be effective . . . [W]e should begin with the honest recognition that the shaping of a consensus among Catholics on the spectrum of life issues is far from finished." Stressing the centrality of dialogue in the abortion controversy, Bernardin acknowledged, "We face the challenge of stating our case, which is shaped in terms of our faith and our religious convictions, in nonreligious terms which others of different faith convictions might find morally persuasive."

THE NON-HIERARCHICAL ORIGINS OF THE CONSISTENT LIFE ETHIC

Bernardin had not originated, but retrieved from the collective consciousness of the pro-life social movement, the phrase *the consistent ethic of life*. Bernardin was its prominent promulgator, not its source. Some in the Catholic Peace Movement were the first to use the phrase "the consistent ethic of life" and to explicitly link opposition to war and abortion. Tom Cornell, one of the founders of the Catholic Peace Fellowship in 1964, said pacifism led to his opposition to both the Vietnam War and abortion. "Catholic pacifists," he explained, "are opposed to war because it is the planned, mass taking of human life for political purposes. . . We are opposed to abortion, euthanasia, capital punishment, and economically enforced starvation also, on the same basis."[12]

The term "consistent ethic" linking oppositions to abortion and war, as well as capital punishment, appeared in Catholic lay activist and intellectual circles very early in the abortion controversy and more than a decade before Bernardin's crystallization of the term. For example, in 1970, Germain Grisez's essay "Toward a Consistent Natural Law Ethics of Killing" appeared in the *American Journal of Jurisprudence* (vol. 15). In 1971, Gordon Zahn, one of the founders of Pax Christi, an international Catholic peace organization committed to nonviolence, wrote an essay using "consistency" and explicitly linking the oppositions to the Vietnam war and abortion: "It is not just a matter of consistency; in a very real sense it is the choice between integrity and hypocrisy. No one who publicly mourns the senseless burning of a napalmed child should be indifferent to the intentional killing of a living fetus in the womb. . . ."[13]

Nor was Bernardin the first Catholic bishop to use the phrase "consistent" for linking abortion, war, and capital punishment oppositions. On July 4, 1971, at St. Patrick's Cathedral at a liturgy for Catholic judges, lawyers and public officials, the late Archbishop Humberto S. Medeiros of Boston gave a homily: "A Call to a Consistent Ethic of Life and the Law." Medeiros preached that opposing abortion required consistency and comprehensiveness including opposing the arms race, militarism, capital punishment, and poverty: "If we are vocal about the rights of innocent life in the womb yet indifferent to the equally innocent life in warfare, we destroy the consistency of our ethical posture: either all life is always sacred, or no segment of life is ever secure from indiscriminate attack." When the American Bishops began their "Respect Life Program" in 1972, they invited Catholics to focus on the "sanctity of life and the many threats to life in the modern world, including violence, hunger and poverty."

A year after Medeiros' homily and a decade before Bernardin's "Consistent Ethic of Life" address, a social movement organization explicitly linked opposing abortion and opposing the American war in Vietnam—the National Youth Pro-life Coalition. The Coalition began the same year as *Roe* and its *Declaration of Purpose* explained its motive: "The Coalition is deeply concerned that our contemporary society is not consistent in its respect for human life." The Coalition challenged those who were "antiabortion, pro-war and pro-capital punishment" to become more consistent because "true conservatism should involve a willingness to 'conserve' all human life."

The Coalition began at the University of Minnesota where any defense of the unborn without linking it to the war in Vietnam and the arms race struck most student bystanders as, if not immature morality, then underdeveloped moral reflection. Susan Hilgers, one of the founders of NYPLC, added that the founders also realized that "by and large, women who were faced with having an abortion often times were first socially aborted by those around her."

Six years after *Roe*, in 1979, Juli Loesch began Pro-lifers for Survival, which linked the oppositions to war and abortion. In 1980, the Evangelical Christian journal *Sojourners* explicitly linked opposition to abortion with its opposition to the arms race and capital punishment. The editors used the term "consistent," adding that they had previously hesitated to make public their abortion opposition because "Like many, we have often been put off by the anti-abortion movement." The editors added, "The truth is that many poor women do not regard abortion as a real solution but as a brutal substitute for social justice and even as white society's way of controlling the population of racial minorities."[14]

Closer to the Bernardin Gannon Lecture, Mary Meehan wrote a November 1980 essay for *Sojourners* entitled "Will Someone Please Be Consistent?" The same issue also contained pro-life statements from Daniel Berrigan and (yes) Jesse Jackson.

Thus, the late Cardinal Joseph Bernardin *crystallized* rather than originated the term "a consistent ethic of life." Even the accompanying phrase "the seamless garment," which Bernardin used during the media interviews following his Gannon address, came from the movement's discourse. The late Eileen Egan, a member of the Catholic Worker and one of the founders of *Pax Christi,* recalled that in exasperation "the word popped out" in conversation with the late English journalist Malcolm Muggeridge, who agreed with her on abortion but not nuclear disarmament.

ANTI-ABORTION TACTICS VERSUS PRO-LIFE IDEALS

The consistent ethic approach was, and is, highly contested within the right-to-life movement. Most mainstream activists rejected it as poor politics. Others were less polite. Judy Brown, the founder and only president of the American Life Lobby, declared that for the movement to take a multi-issue approach would be to "commit hari kari." James McFadden, the late publisher of *The Human Life Review,* complained Bernardin's "many issues approach still cloaks pro-abort Catholic politicians" like Edward Kennedy, Geraldine

Ferraro, Mario Cuomo, and Patrick Leahy who vote for poverty programs and military cuts but are pro-choice. James Hitchcock wrote in *The Human Life Review* that if voters took Bernardin seriously, they would have no one to vote for.

But, as they say in politics, there is no free lunch. The Reagan embrace of the mainstream right-to-life movement, which brought abortion opponents into the White House with its powers of court appointments and policy impacts, had its costs. It derailed some clear movements toward consistency even within the mainstream movement. Less than five years before the Reagan candidacy, editor Jane Grant in the September 1974 edition of the *National Right to Life News* characterized legal abortion supporters as mostly wealthy upper class elites whose notion of equality stopped at equal access to abortion: "The rich want to 'share' abortion with the poor. But 'sharing' stops when it comes to wealth, clubs and neighborhoods." After Reagan, the careful reader of *National Right to Life News* finds no similar comment. A year earlier (*NRL News*, February 1973) Donna M. Sullivan urged readers to ask those supporting legal abortion, "Are social pressures now geared more to getting rid of poor babies than assisting their mothers with their economic problems?" She added that when abortion opponents oppose using tax money for Medicaid-funded abortions, "we are really saying that even if it costs us more to help those who cannot help themselves, we are willing to spend more, if necessary, so long as it is spent to foster and sustain life."

The Reagan embrace with its promise of Republican support came to restrain the deep egalitarian attitudes of the multitude of ordinary people of the movement opposing abortion. Nevertheless, nowhere in movement literature is there expressed any preference for Republican signature economic policies, such as tax cuts or cuts in social programs. Indeed, a familiar movement theme is criticism of the Reagan administration for putting abortion on the "backburner" while administration leaders righted the economy. In an article for *Sisterlife*, the predecessor of *The American Feminist*, Jane Thomas-Bailey wrote, "Nor are most pro-lifers die-hard right-wingers. Most are relatively apolitical, formerly apathetic people who have suddenly been galvanized on the issue of abortion. If you told many of them that the best way to stop abortion was to join the Socialist Workers party, they would do so without blinking. What happens is that as they become active, the right wing welcomes them with open arms while the left wing tells them to take a long walk off a short pier. They identify with the right wing because they are offered no alternative."[15]

In later addresses, Bernardin endeavored to answer tactics-oriented critics and invited them to consider ways of showing the long-term, transformative pro-life aspiration even as they sought tactical ways to influence election results and affect abortion laws. In his March 11, 1984, address at St. Louis University, "A Consistent Ethic of Life: Continuing the Dialogue," Bernardin assured critics that the consistent ethic did not make "quality of life" and "right-to-life" issues morally equivalent. Nor did he think it wrong for movement activists to focus on abortion: "It is not necessary or possible for every person to engage in each issue." Still, "the way we oppose one threat should be related to support for a systemic vision of life" because "there is, I maintain, a political and psychological linkage among the life issues—from war to welfare concerns—which we ignore at our own peril. A systemic vision of life seeks to expand the moral imagination of a society, not partition it into airtight categories."

EQUALITY AND CLASS

A highly respected social science research on abortion is Kristin Luker's 1984 book, *Abortion and the Politics of Motherhood.* The majority of sociologists share her thesis the abortion debate "is so passionate and hard-fought *because it is a referendum on the place and meaning of motherhood*"[16] with feminists and housewives forming the major competing camps. But Luker fails to incorporate into her "politics of motherhood" thesis—feminist equality progressives versus traditionalist gender conservatives—what she herself empirically found as the core of pro-life concern: the moral intuition that abortion does not serve but subverts equality:

> The pro-life movement will also eventually have to come to terms... with abortion intended to prevent the birth of a deformed child. According to public opinion polls, such abortions are acceptable to more than four-fifths of the American public. However, compared with the other two cases (life of the mother, incest and rape), this one is the least ideologically tolerable for pro-life people. Many of the pro-life activists we interviewed were ambivalent about abortions to save the life of the mother, and a few were ambivalent in the cases of rape or incest, but there was no ambivalence at all about the case of "fetal indications."
>
> On the surface, this appears strange: opinion polls seem to suggest that the general public accepts abortion in this case as "necessary" rather than "discretionary." But abortions for fetal deformity cut to the deepest level of

> pro-life feelings about "selective" abortion. Because the logic of abortion in this case depends upon a judgment that the embryo is "damaged" in one respect or another, it suggests to pro-life people an acceptance of the idea that humans can be ranked along some scale of perfection and that people who fall below a certain arbitrary standard can be excluded.[17]

Luker is a good researcher and carefully records what she hears her pro-life interviewees tell her about their radical sense of equality; then, she absorbs and subordinates this radical element into her own story line about the division between pro-life traditionalist women and pro-choice progressive feminist women. Similarly, Luker found, "On almost every social background variable we examined, pro-life and pro-choice women differed dramatically. For example, in terms of income, almost half of all pro-life women in this study reported an income of less than $20,000 a year, but only one-fourth of the pro-choice women reported an income that low, and a considerable portion of these were young women just starting their careers."[18]

But even reviewers who highlight the significance of social class differences among abortion protagonists fail to note the radical egalitarianism expressed by pro-life activists. In his review, Peter Berger writes, "For the sociologist, Luker's data shout a single word: class! Put simply, class is the single most important variable predicting an individual's attitude toward abortion. This suggests, however, a further sociological hypothesis—that the debate over abortion is part and parcel of a larger class conflict."[19] Remarkably, Berger offers little reflection on the long-term significance of a flourishing pro-life movement for the aspiration toward a more equal and just society. Similarly, the late Christopher Lasch wrote that Luker's study shows that abortion is "first and foremost a class issue." He then said, "These differences defined the difference between two social classes, each with its own view of the world—the one eager to press its recent gains and to complete the modern revolution of rising expectations, the other devoted to a last-ditch defense of the 'forgotten American.' "[20]

Thus Luker and her most prominent reviewers do not reflect about what movement activists themselves say about their abortion opposition and its connection with the roots of an authentic equality. Lasch senses that something deeper is at stake when activists talk about the right to life of even "defective" fetuses, but like Luker, he subordinates these unfamiliar data to the familiar conservative countermovement story line and consigns his intuition to a footnote on page 90: "These fears are by no means fanciful or exaggerated" and cites the 1970 *Journal of the California Medical Association* which "welcomed the growing acceptance of abortion as a prototype of what is to occur, the harbinger of a 'new ethic' that would substitute the quality of life, in effect, for the sanctity of life."[21]

FROM COUNTER TO TRANSFORMATIVE MOVEMENT

With the gradual disengagement from the beguiling but implausible promise begun during the Reagan era that moral conservativism could find a political home among free market conservatives, movement activists, bystanders, and scholars are now better positioned to recognize the label "anti-abortion" applied only to the beginning of the pro-life movement. Its pioneers intuitively knew that in time, laws making killing the unborn a right would slowly eclipse the human conscience and impede the hallowed aspiration to transform societies into communities of nonviolence that valued all humans.

NOTES AND REFERENCES

1. Melich, Tanya. 1996. *The Republican War against Women.* New York: Bantam.
2. Ibid., p. 335.
3. Ibid., p. 38.
4. Kmiec, Douglas W. 1992. *The Attorney General's Lawyer.* Westport, CT: Praeger, chapter 4.
5. Critchlow, Donald T. 1999. *Intended Consequences: Birth Control, Abortion, and the Federal Government in Modern America.* New York: Oxford University Press, p. 291, n. 100.
6. Francome, Colin. 1984. *Abortion Freedom: A Worldwide Movement.* London: George Allen and Unwin, p. 210.
7. Morrison, Robert G. 1998. "Breakfasting with Champions," *Life and Learning VIII* (proceedings of the University Faculty for Life Conference), pp. 196–197; for an update, see Kelly, James R. September 27, 2004. A Catholic Votes for John Kerry. *America,* 13–17.
8. Alberoni, Francesco. 1984. *Movement and Institution,* tr. by Patricia E. Delmore. New York: Columbia University Press, pp. 316–317.
9. Critchlow, *Intended Consequences,* p. 235.
10. Fuechtman, T. G. 1988. *Consistent Ethic of Life: Joseph Cardinal Bernardin.* Chicago: Loyola University Press, pp. 1–11.
11. National Council of Catholic Bishops. 1983. *The Challenge to Peace.* Washington, D.C.: Author, paragraphs 286, 287.
12. McNeal, Patricia. 1992. *Harder Than War: Catholic Peacemaking in Twentieth-Century America.* New Jersey, NJ: Rutgers University Press, p. 169.
13. Zahn, Gordon. May 28, 1971. The Unborn Life and the Protection of Life. *Commonweal,* 337–339.

14. *Sojourners.* November 1980. Vol. 9, No. 11.
15. Thomas-Bailey, Jane. Fall 1985. Prolifers Playing Trivial Pursuit: A Call to Action. *Sisterlife*, 3.
16. Luker, Kristin. 1984. *Abortion and the Politics of Motherhood.* Berkeley: The University of California Press, p. 193. [Emphasis in original]
17. Ibid., p. 236.
18. Ibid., p. 194.
19. Berger, Peter. April 30, 1984. "Life Choices: A Review of Kristin Luker, Abortion and the Politics of Motherhood." *The New Republic*, pp. 35–39.
20. Lasch, Christopher. 1991. *The True and Only Heaven: Progress and Its Critics.* New York: W. W. Norton, p. 491.
21. Ibid., p. 492.

Connecting the Dots—Nonviolently

Michael N. Nagler

> *"In so far as specific problems are being tackled by authorities as though they were separate problems, there can be no lasting cures for any of them."*
>
> —*Richard Burton*

While World War II raged, Mahatma Gandhi grimly predicted that the Allies would prevail but would become more brutal than Hitler because they used his methods. At the time, it seemed to many an impossible exaggeration, but with the United States using torture at Guantánamo and Iraq, and more importantly with brazen attempts to bestow the imprimatur of law, Gandhi's prediction seems uncomfortably prophetic. We can better understand it by framing the point simply: Behind every modern problem, violence is the root cause and nonviolence the solution.

Real violence lies not in the act but in the *intention* to injure. Every mature spiritual tradition has held that the damage is done by the intention itself: "You have heard how it was said to our ancestors: You must not kill.... But I say this to you, that anyone who is angry with a brother or sister will answer for it" (Matthew 5:21). The UNESCO Charter states that "war begins in the minds" of men and women. We have not learned to use that perdurable wisdom, so we find ourselves dabbing at a symptom here and there without reducing the overall cause—or worse, without grasping the connection between means and ends, actually increasing it.

This also applies to violence we commit unconsciously or *structural violence*—Johan Galtung's widely used term for exploitation built into a social system. Structural violence is the motivating force for globalization, but it is not new. The Buddha's definition of a nonviolent person is one who "does not kill *nor cause to kill.*"

Most approaches to violence currently practiced are a failure. Our approach to crime has put more people in prison while barely denting the crime rate. Our approach to world peace leads to a series of wars; in Iraq we are "breeding terrorists faster than we can kill them,"[1] while at home the "war on drugs" (actually, a war on drug users and dealers) continues as a costly, violent failure. Preventing murder with the death penalty, inasmuch as it has any effect, more likely encourages murder by modeling killing as a problem solver. The access to abortion which was supposed to liberate women and prevent abuse of unwanted children has facilitated callousness toward the needs of pregnant women, while child abuse rates have skyrocketed.

To understand the dynamic, we must also realize that the wish to harm others harms oneself. St. Augustine said, "[H]ow could anyone imagine that his *enemy* could do him as much damage as his *enmity*?" Nonviolence begins in inner struggle; the struggle against enmity and to keep anger, fear, and greed from having sway over us. This has immense benefits and leads to an exhilarating sense of purpose.[2]

CRIME AND PERSONAL VIOLENCE

Crime does not arise, as in cartoons, from evil villains out of nowhere, but has causes. For example, there is a class of unfortunates known as sexual predators. The rise of this and other sexual crime is directly keyed to the rise of sexual advertising, sexually explicit "entertainment" and other mores. The connection is rarely invoked in public debate about reducing unwanted sexual behavior. Advertising, and hence the economies of industrial societies, depends on stimulation. Instead, various coercive measures are increased to contain the behavior of these predators, like posting their names and whereabouts on websites and forbidding them to frequent places with children. The result "is as we create all these new obstacles we may be making them more dangerous."[3]

Yet this generally applies to crime. That is the trouble with our search for security; we are "making terrorists faster than we can kill them" at home and abroad.

Crime has reached enormous proportions in the industrialized world. A shocking failure stands revealed in the prevalence of violent behavior, the tremendous insecurity we experience, and the incarceration and recidivism of criminals that has disfigured life, all because we fight one form of violence—crime—with another—retribution.

Modern researchers recognize that Gandhi's program called *Nai Talim* (new education) is an antidote to criminality, because access to education is the single most effective form of prevention of crime. It can also be restorative, as many experiences with offenders have demonstrated. Yet, with so many people already lured into criminal behavior by the popular culture and caught up in the criminal justice system, we must also consider what nonviolence can offer to deal with these people justly and rationally, healing rather than exacerbating their alienation.

The criminal justice system is "an expensive, unjust, immoral failure."[4] "The more we have reacted to crime," says Richard Quinney, "the further we have removed ourselves from any understanding and any reduction of the problem."[5] Our behavior is a reaction; we are hurt, we hurt back. The death penalty is but the most extreme form.

The nonviolent response is called *restorative,* not *retributive,* justice. Harold Pepinsky spells out the difference:

> In decades of sampling millennia of literature across traditions, . . . I see everyone applying one of just two social control systems: peacemaking, or what I call "warmaking." In the context of governmental efforts to control domestic social disorder, Ruth Morris calls "warmaking" "the retributive justice system." . . . When one chooses to make war on a social problem rather than to make peace with it, one adopts this system of thought: The first order of business is to identify and assess blame against those personally responsible for the danger and insecurity we face; these are our enemies. Next we try to isolate them and subdue them—stamping out the enemy's will to fight. . . .
>
> If you decide to regard threatening social disorder in the peacemaking social control system, blame gets in the way of cleaning up the social mess and restoring antagonists' capacity to get along safely together . . . the preeminent task of the peacemaker is to *weave combatants, weakest victims first, back into a social fabric of mutual trust, mutual safety, mutual security.*[6]

This "new" way of thinking (actually, it was widely practiced in some indigenous societies) has a pragmatic principle behind it. Jeremy Bentham said "Sanguinary laws have a tendency to render men cruel, either by fear, by imitation, or by revenge, while laws dictated by mildness humanize the manners of a nation and the spirit of government."[7] (For more on restorative justice, see www.restorativejustice.org.)

POVERTY

Gandhi's bold economic vision rests on one principle: *trusteeship.*[8] Trusteeship, or stewardship, is the nonviolent equivalent of ownership. A trustee is responsible for, but does not personally own, any asset over which he or she has some control—including nonmaterial assets like talents and skills. The sense of possession (an illusion, according to the wisdom tradition in which Gandhi stands) leads to an economy of *wants*; the sense of responsibility leads instead to an economy of *needs*. Needs can be satisfied; wants cannot. Trusteeship would thus enable us to convert humanity from materialism to a sane economic order in which poverty, among other violent things, would disappear in due course.

WAR

How is the antidote of nonviolence applied to war? Gandhi said, "[N]onviolence that merely offers civil resistance to the authorities and goes no further scarcely deserves the name." He began to create nonviolent mechanisms to address wars. Two such mechanisms have evolved.

The first is called Civilian-Based Defense (CBD). It is carried out by civilians defending their society—as opposed to their borders—against either foreign invasion (as in the Prague Spring uprising of 1968–1969) or an internal coup (as against the Kapp Putsch of 1920). Gene Sharp and other contributors to nonviolence literature have described these episodes and others like them very well.[9] Some organizations have formed to promote CBD, and some enlightened governments (mainly in northern Europe) have even made provisions for this form of defense alongside conventional methods.

The other format where nonviolence resists war has taken off more dramatically, furnishing even more actual experience with modest versions of the principle: Third Party Nonviolent Intervention (TPNI). Third parties, often internationals from far away, intervene to provide services like rumor abatement, witnessing, good offices, protective accompaniment (some of the most effective organizations specialize in this), election monitoring, and ultimately, if all else fails, actual interpositioning between conflicting parties. Surprising as it may sound to the uninitiated, a third party can break up the polarized dynamic of an intense conflict. By representing peace by their very presence, and the risk it entails (not to mention creating practical difficulties for combatants), it can derail the otherwise seemingly unstoppable slide into war. The slowly accumulating history of nonviolence reveals that this type of intervention has a surprisingly good track record as both an effective and a relatively safe thing to do.[10]

CONCLUSION

René Girard has shown how "unanimous violence," or "scapegoating," is an ancient mechanism by which societies protect themselves from runaway violence, which has been known to obliterate entire cultures. A group threatened by social chaos will focus on a single person or group to be unanimously blamed for the disaster and be "purged." This is the main social function of bigotry. From time immemorial, this has been an irrational but effective way to limit the damage of human destructiveness in the short term—until the next buildup of divisive tensions. Its origins shrouded deep in antiquity, the reaction lives on in many institutions ranging from animal sacrifice through gladiatorial combat to the death penalty in modern cultures. There have even been suggestions in explicitly neo-pagan literature of abortion as a form of child sacrifice to the goddess Artemis![11]

One of Girard's insights is that compassion-based monotheistic religions represent a decisive breakthrough in human moral awareness because the founders overturn blood sacrifice and the blind societal violence it thus encodes. One of the most violent cultural forms of our age, the Christian Zionism segment of the "rapture" cult explicitly calls for a return to animal sacrifice in the restored temple in Jerusalem![12]

Could we not forge narratives toward a more humane and safer way of dealing with crises? There is ample evidence that groups in "common predicament" can respond with organization and altruism. This is from Dr. Ryan, after Hurricane Katrina:

> [E]veryone in the hospital experienced something that the national news failed to convey; it was not chaos, mass confusion or hopelessness. Rather, it became a sense of teamwork combined with determination to save these patients and to get everyone to safety . . . There was no air-conditioning and the stairwells were over 100 degrees. However, nobody complained, nobody took a break. Everyone was focused on the goal of saving the patients, and everything else was of no concern.[13]

Unlike unanimous violence, unanimous nonviolence has a high survival value, with long-term positive change.

As Dan Baum wrote in the *New Yorker*, veterans returning from Iraq are far more traumatized by the injuries they have inflicted on others than those inflicted on themselves[14] We in peace studies have long known about this very human response, which Rachel MacNair has termed Perpetration Induced Traumatic Stress.[15] This is welcome evidence of the regenerative potential in human beings that we have long been arguing for. It *is* possible to build a nonviolent future.

NOTES AND REFERENCES

1. Often heard from Zbiniew Brezinscki and other policy analysts by Jack Duvall, reporting in the recent conference on War, Peace, and the Media, Portland, OR, June 2005.
2. Nagler, Michael. 2003. *The Search for a Nonviolent Future.* Makawao, HI: Inner Ocean. Some passages in the present chapter appeared in *Search.*
3. *Santa Rosa Press Democrat,* November 12, 2005, p. A5.
4. Morris, Ruth. 1995. *Penal Abolition: The Practical Choice.* Toronto: Canadian Scholars Press, p. 5.
5. Pepinsky, Harold and Richard Quinney, eds. 1991. *Criminology as Peacemaking.* Bloomington: Indiana University, p. 3.
6. From the syllabus of Prof. Pepinsky's course, CJUS P202, "Alternative Social Control Systems," Spring 1996. [Emphasis added]
7. Bowring, John, ed.. 1843. *The Works of Jeremy Bentham,* Vol. 2. Edinburgh: W. Tait, p. 562.
8. A good place to start is Diwan, Romesh and Mark Lutz. 1987. *Essays in Gandhian Economics.* New York: IT Development Group.
9. Sharp, Gene. 1985. *National Security through Civilian-Based Defense.* Omaha, NE: Association for Transarmament Studies; Sharp, Gene (1985). *Making Europe Unconquerable.* Cambridge, MA: Ballinger.
10. Boardman, Elizabeth. 2005. *Taking a Stand: A Guide to Peace Teams and Accompaniment Projects.* Gabriola Island, BC, Canada: New Society.
11. Peterson, Brenda. Sister against Sister, September–October 1993. *New Age Journal;* Paris, Ginette. 1992. *The Sacrament of Abortion.* Woodstock, CT: Spring Publications, pp. 25–27; 13; Paris, Ginette. 1986. *Pagan Meditations.* Woodstock, CT: Spring Publications, p. 148.
12. For example, see Halsell, Grace. 1999. *Forcing God's Hand: Why Millions Pray for a Quick Rapture—And the Destruction of Planet Earth.* Beltsville, MD: The Whitley Company, p. 69.
13. Shannon, Ryan. October 17, 2005. *The Times Picayune.*
14. Baum, Dan. July 12 and 19, 2004. The Price of Valor. *New Yorker Magazine,* http://www.newyorker.com/archive/2004/07/12/040712fa_fact (accessed December 19, 2007).
15. MacNair, Rachel M. 2002. *Perpetration-Induced Traumatic Stress: The Psychological Consequences of Killing.* Westport, CT: Praeger. See also Chapter 5 of this book.

18

People Power and Regime Change: How Nonviolence Spreads Democracy

Stephen Zunes

> *"Everyone knows that the fire from a little spark will increase and blaze ever higher as long as it finds wood to burn; yet without being quenched by water, but merely by finding no more fuel to feed on, it consumes itself, dies down, and is no longer in flame. Similarly, the more tyrants pillage, the more they crave, the more they ruin and destroy—the more one yields to them, and obeys them, by that much do they become mightier and more formidable, the readier to annihilate and destroy. But if not one thing is yielded to them, if without any violence they are simply not obeyed, they become naked and undone and as nothing."*
>
> —*Étienne de la Boétie, 1548*

Those who defend war, abortion, the death penalty, and other forms of violence often rationalize their positions by claiming such violence prevents greater suffering. Supporters of capital punishment claim—long refuted by empirical research—that it deters murderers, when the focus should instead be upon such nonviolent preventative measures as gun control, greater economic justice, and improved access to psychological services. Supporters of legalized abortion claim that the disruption to a mother's life from an unwanted pregnancy is of greater moral consequence than the life of the unborn child, when the focus should instead be upon such nonviolent alternatives as adequate support for children and parents or creating conditions that provide women real choices prior to conception.

Revolutionaries trying to justify armed struggle—and the U.S. government defending its invasion of Iraq—claim their violence was necessary to rid oppressed peoples of dictators and provide freedom. Yet, though—like murder and unwanted pregnancies—dictatorships are a serious problem, seeking to overcome them through violence not only raises serious moral issues, but generally makes a bad situation worse.

Fortunately, there is a clear alternative to both military intervention and armed revolution in promoting "regime change" and advancing the cause of freedom which has proven quite effective: nonviolent action.

Nonviolent action campaigns have been part of political life for millennia, challenging abuses by authorities, spearheading social reforms, and protesting militarism and discrimination. In more recent years, there has been a dramatic growth in popular nonviolent movements for political and social reforms, in some cases, even toppling repressive regimes.

Primarily nonviolent "people power" movements overthrew authoritarian regimes in nearly two dozen countries over the past three decades and forced substantial reforms in over thirty others. Even the relatively conservative group Freedom House, in its detailed 2005 empirical study *How Freedom Is Won*, concluded that the use of nonviolent action by democratic civil society organizations was by far the single most important factor in the dramatic growth of democratic governance worldwide.

Nonviolence has shown its power to bring down dictatorships from Mongolia to Madagascar, Czechoslovakia to Bolivia, and from Serbia to the Philippines despite immense differences in culture, religion, level of development, and the regime's ideological orientation.

In contrast to armed struggles, these are movements of organized popular resistance to government authority which eschew weapons of modern warfare. Unlike conventional political movements, nonviolent campaigns usually employ tactics outside the mainstream political processes of electioneering and lobbying such as strikes, boycotts, mass demonstrations, the popular contestation of public space, tax refusal, destruction of symbols of government authority (such as official identification cards), refusal to obey official orders (such as curfew restrictions), and creation of alternative institutions.

WHY NONVIOLENCE WORKS

The growing appreciation of the power of nonviolence comes from increasing acknowledgment of the damage from armed struggle. Increasing costs from counterinsurgency warfare due to displacement of the population, destruction of farms and villages, damage to national infrastructure, collapse of the economy, and devastation of the environment led many to question whether, even with eventual victory, it is worth the costs.

Another problem is the tendency, once in power, for victorious armed movements against dictatorships to fail in establishing pluralistic, democratic, and independent political systems supporting development and promoting human rights. Armed struggle often promotes the ethos of a secret elite vanguard, downplaying democracy and showing less tolerance for pluralism. Often disagreements that could be resolved peaceably in nonmilitarized institutions lead to bloody factional fighting. Some countries, like Algeria and Guinea-Bissau, experienced military coups soon after armed movements ousted colonialists. Others, like Angola and Mozambique, endured bloody civil wars.

Poverty and injustices afflicting many countries suffering under dictatorships are so extensive that a successful armed movement is not sufficient to address the pressing concerns facing a country in transition after the devastation of the revolution. Therefore, there is growing interest in tactics that minimize dislocation and maximize the chances for people to become contributing members of a postauthoritarian political order.

Insurgents are increasingly convinced that armed resistance tends to upset undecided people. A government facing a violent insurgency can justify its repression. But violence used against unarmed resistance movements usually creates greater sympathy for the opponents, a phenomenon which sociologist Gene Sharp has called "political jiu-jitsu." An opposition movement leverages state repression to advance the movement's ends.

Unarmed campaigns can also engage far more participants, taking advantage of the popular support pro-democracy movements engender. Unarmed resistance encourages the creation of alternative institutions which further undermines the repressive status quo and forms the basis for a new democratic order.

Armed resistance often backfires by legitimizing the use of repressive tactics. Violence from the opposition is often welcomed by authoritarian governments and even encouraged through the use of agents provocateurs, because it justifies repression. But state violence unleashed on unarmed dissidents often triggers a turning point in nonviolent struggles. A government attack against peaceful demonstrators can be the spark needed to transform periodic protests into a full-scale insurrection.

Unarmed resistance movements also tend to sow divisions within pro-government circles. Disagreements surface internally, since few governments are as prepared to deal with unarmed revolts as to quash armed ones. Violent repression of a peaceful movement can alter popular and elite perceptions of the power's legitimacy. Some pro-government elements may become less concerned about consequences of a compromise with insurgents if their resistance is nonviolent. Unarmed movements increase the likelihood of defections and noncooperation by unmotivated police and military personnel, whereas armed revolts legitimize the government's coercive apparatus, enhancing its self-perception as the civil society's protector. The moral power of nonviolence is crucial to the ability of an opposition movement to reframe the perceptions of key parties: the public, political elites, and the military, most of whom have no difficulty supporting violence against violent insurrections.

The efficacy of nonviolent resistance in dividing supporters of the status quo is apparent not just in rendering government troops less effective but also in challenging the attitudes of an entire nation and even foreign actors, as in the South African struggle against apartheid. Pictures of peaceful protesters—including whites, clergy members, and other "upstanding citizens"—broadcast on television worldwide lent legitimacy to antiapartheid forces and undermined the South African government in a way armed rebellion could not. As nonviolent resistance within the country escalated, external pressure with economic sanctions and other solidarity tactics by the international community raised the costs of maintaining the apartheid system.

The nonlocal audience may be just as important as the immediate community. Gandhi tried to appeal to British citizens in Manchester and London, and organizers of the civil rights movement in the U.S. South communicated to the entire nation. Insurgency against the Soviet bloc was disseminated by television spreading the news, legitimating local protests that no longer seemed like isolated events. The prominent role of the global media during the anti-Marcos "people power" movement in 1986 was instrumental in forcing the U.S. government to diminish support for the Philippine dictator. Israeli repression of nonviolent protests by Palestinians during the 1980s had a similar effect on Americans. As Rashid Khalidi observed, the Palestinians had "succeeded at last in conveying the reality of their victimization to world public opinion."

Creating alternative structures provides a moral and practical underpinning for bringing about social change. Parallel structures may render state control increasingly impotent, as they did throughout Eastern Europe leading to the 1989 events. In the Philippines, Marcos lost power not through defeat of his troops but from withdrawal of support for his authority. The same day Marcos was officially sworn in, Corazon Aquino was symbolically sworn in as the people's president. Most Filipinos saw Marcos's election as fraudulent; the vast majority offered allegiance to President Aquino instead. The transfer of allegiance from one authority to another makes the physical seizure of power by force unnecessary.

Using nonviolence to overthrow dictatorships and establish democracy appears to impact popular attitudes toward violence overall. In virtually every country that has had a successful nonviolent insurrection against an autocratic regime, the new democratic government has abolished the death penalty, dramatically reduced military spending, and passed stronger environmental laws. In former dictatorships where minority groups were legally discriminated against, such laws were overturned. Some of these new democracies have imposed greater restrictions on abortion, while virtually none have liberalized abortion laws.

As with violent revolutions, not all nonviolent revolutions have emerged victorious. Such movements in Burma and China, for example, were successfully repressed. Nevertheless, the track record of nonviolent action against repressive governments is impressive.

THE ROLE OF THE UNITED STATES

As a belated effort to rationalize the invasion of Iraq, the U.S. administration has increasingly stressed the need for "regime change" to promote democracy and has even tried to take credit for the dramatic growth of democratic governments in recent decades. Some critics of U.S. foreign policy have even accused the United States of staging "soft coups" through successful nonviolent uprisings in Serbia, Georgia and Ukraine. In reality, these movements were homegrown and owed their successes to the courage and innovation of their own people. The United States was no more responsible for nonviolent revolutions of Eastern Europe than the Soviet Union was responsible for violent revolutions in Central America.

Furthermore, nonviolent movements have ousted at least as many pro-American dictators as anti-American dictators: Duvalier in Haiti, Marcos in the Philippines, Chun in South Korea, and Pinochet in Chile, among others.

During the Cold War, U.S. support for right-wing dictatorships was justified by claiming they were an important bulwark against communism, which was deemed impossible to reform from within. It was felt military means through strategic alliances like NATO and armed insurgencies like the Afghan mujahedeen were the only way left-wing dictatorships could be challenged. Yet, nonviolent movements eventually brought down entrenched communist rulers in Poland, East Germany, Czechoslovakia, Hungary, and Mongolia. During the same period, the Baltic states of Lithuania, Latvia, and Estonia broke free from the Soviet Union, also largely through the use of nonviolent resistance.

Could the Iraqis, left to their own devices, have toppled Saddam Hussein and thereby brought democracy without the bloodshed and chaos of the U.S. invasion? Quite possibly. Indonesia's Suharto—who ruled the world's largest Muslim nation for over thirty-three years—had even more blood on his hands than Saddam. Yet he was forced from power in a largely nonviolent uprising in 1998. Largely nonviolent insurrections have also toppled tyrannical leaders of other Muslim states, like the Shah of Iran in 1979, Sudan's Jafaar Numeiri in 1985, Bangladesh's General Ershad in 1990 and Mali's Moussa Traore in 1991. Islam has traditionally emphasized a kind of social contract between the ruler and his subjects which gives the people the right, and even the obligation, to refuse to cooperate with authorities seen as unjust.

Ironically, in Iraq, it was the United States, Great Britain, and other Western nations that may have made the emergence of such nonviolent movements impossible. Most of the world's successful nonviolent pro-democracy movements have centered in the urban middle class and industrial working class. In Iraq, however, thanks to the devastation to the country's civilian infrastructure during the bombing campaign in the 1991 Gulf War and the debilitating sanctions that followed, the once burgeoning middle and skilled working classes were reduced to extreme poverty or forced to emigrate. In their place emerged a new class of black marketeers with a strong stake in preserving the status quo. Furthermore, the sanctions not only had serious humanitarian consequences—resulting in the deaths of hundreds of thousands of Iraqis from malnutrition and preventable diseases—but actually strengthened Saddam Hussein's grip on power. By being forced to depend on the regime for badly needed rations like food, medicine, and other necessities, the Iraqis became even less likely to challenge it.

Whether the 2003 U.S. invasion was motivated in part to bring democracy to Iraq or if it was simply a rationalization to justify an imperialist quest for oil and strategic standing in the Middle East, the violent overthrow of Saddam Hussein's regime has brought more violence and misery to the people of Iraq. While the moral imperative and strategic importance of bringing down the world's remaining dictatorships is real, attempting to do so through violence will only bring about more suffering. It is the application of massive strategic nonviolent action by the peoples of these countries themselves that will eventually allow freedom to triumph.

RESOURCES

For Web resources that include books, films, and even a computer game on nonviolent strategy, see www.aforcemorepowerful.org; the series of "A Force More Powerful" includes a book, the game, and a Public Broadcasting series of that name. The most recent works of Gene Sharp and colleagues can be found at www.aeinstein.org, including translations into other languages. Other resources can be found at the Web site for the International Center on Nonviolent Conflict, www.nonviolent-conflict.org. The coeditors of this volume have produced books on this topic: *Nonviolent Social Movements: A Geographic Perspective* (Blackwell, 1999), edited by Stephen Zunes, Lester R. Kurtz, and Sarah Beth Asher, and *History Shows: Winning with Nonviolent Action*, by Rachel MacNair (www.xlibris.com/HistoryShows).

Conflict Transformation: Dissolving "Battle Lines"

Rachel M. MacNair

REARRANGING THE FURNITURE IN PEOPLE'S HEADS

The brother and sister both want the orange. They squabble about it incessantly. It turns out the brother wants to eat the inside, the sister wants the rind to make marmalade. The solution is now obvious.

This classic example from conflict resolution pioneer Mary Parker Follett in 1940[1] illustrates dealing with conflict more constructively than with win-lose or compromise. We look at the difference between *positions* and *interests*. The siblings each had the *position* of wanting the orange. Once this was broken down into *interests*, both could be satisfied.

Battle lines give winners and losers. Otherwise, compromises are negotiated. These happen constantly in politics, seen as virtuous since they avoid bloodshed. But when conflicts are transformed by getting past positions and considering interests, creative solutions are often found. Then everyone is satisfied. Otherwise, the parties might spoil for a rematch.

This approach can get complicated, requiring much skill, practice, and patience. Calming down and remembering that people are people and not competing camps requires breaking habits imposed by a competition-oriented society. Yet, as more people learn the basic skills of conflict resolution, or better yet, transforming conflict into creative problem-solving, the more peaceful the society becomes.

So far, this is Peace Studies 101, Lesson 1. Nobody studies conflict resolution skills without learning this lesson. Such concepts form the foundation of these skills.

How sad that peace advocates, or related people such as feminists, often forget this basic point, or never learned it. The cry "the battle lines are drawn" means establishing concepts like "winning" or "losing." Any social movement starting out as the underdog usually loses. The way for such movements to "win" is by dispensing with the win-lose model.

THE DOVE NEEDS BOTH WINGS TO FLY

What do "right-wing" and "left-wing" mean? Originally, wings of the French parliament. The right-wingers divided people into races or nations and thought their own to be the best. Left-wingers divided people into economic classes instead, and rather than approving they thought such divisions should be dissolved. Hence, the left-wingers believed in human equality. In those terms, the pro-war people are likely to be right-wing, and the peace movement finds its natural home in the left-wing. But under the original division, *both* pro-life and pro-choice movements are left-wing, at least in their foundational principles.

What do the wings mean *now*? Are they the same as conservatives and liberals? When I was growing up, that was the difference between those who do not want change and those who do. Especially since the 1980s, these features have often been reversed. Does it mean that these terms now respectively indicate those who want the government to stay out of our business versus those who want the government to solve our problems? That was how Ronald Reagan presented the difference, but he advocated high military expenses, strong prisons, and capital punishment. His rhetoric of limited government was itself limited.

I have asked several audiences what the coherent principle separating the wings is. So far, nobody knows.

But the wings are positions, not interests. Worse, they bunch positions together. People who classify themselves either way are a wild hodgepodge of different positions. They tend to belong to a set, but deviations are common: Liberals and radicals who oppose abortion and conservatives who favor it; conservatives who oppose the death penalty because no self-respecting pro-lifer trusts a judge with life-or-death decisions; liberal officeholders who push for specific wars; fiscal conservatives versus social conservatives versus pro-business libertarians; and people with secular and religious differences in both wings. For some, the biggest influence on how they self-identify is how their friends and family identify themselves.

So we need to get past the "wing" people belong to, to see specific positions. For dissolving battle lines, we need to consider interests underlying those positions and how they can be addressed. Many interests—protecting women from back-alley butchers, defending countries from attacks or citizens from criminal murder, preventing suffering in the terminally ill—are completely reasonable. Getting past positions and to the interests behind them often leads to useful dialog and creative policy proposals.

INTEGRATING THE CULTURE OF PEACE AND THE CULTURE OF LIFE

The "culture of peace" means society-wide practices and habits promoting peace, a positive view of peace as much more than mere absence of war. The United Nations officially declared 2001–2010 the International Decade for a Culture of Peace. This includes a pledge signed by millions worldwide. The first two of the six things pledged are: "Respect the life and dignity of each human being without discrimination or prejudice" and "Practice active nonviolence, rejecting violence in all its forms . . . in particular towards the most deprived and vulnerable such as children and adolescents." There is a logic that these two be first; they are foundational to peace. They are also the starting points for the "culture of life."

While the term "culture of life" is broadly used to promote protection of individual human lives, it has an official usage promoted by Pope John Paul II. It has become common in Catholic groups, especially conservative ones, and has expanded to non-Catholic conservative groups and politicians. The pope also included death penalty opposition in this definition.

In the polarizing presentation of groups such as the media, the culture of peace has been seen as left-wing and the culture of life as right-wing. Therefore, both get seen as mere propaganda terms. Dr. Jack Willke told me in his diocese that the "Peace and Justice" office and the "Respect Life" office do not get along well with each other.

With common foundational principles, the integration of the culture of peace and the culture of life faces only one obstacle: how embedded they are in the left-wing/right-wing dichotomy. Considering the stereotypes each of these wings inflicts on the other, and groups such as the media inflict on both, this is not a minor point.

An example of how this integration can work is provided by conservative Republican U.S. Senator Sam Brownback of Kansas. In 2005, in an article about the Terri Schiavo case, Gloria Borger quoted him as telling her, "If we're trying to establish a culture of life, it's difficult to have the state sponsoring executions."[2]

I often use this quotation in a group of peace movement people, and they vigorously agree. They can see the inconsistency. They enjoy criticizing people they disagree with and exult in having such people notice the inconsistency in promoting greater reflection on peace and death penalty issues.

But consistency between two things, by definition, has to go both ways. If we're trying to establish a culture of peace, it is difficult to have the state authorizing feticide.

THE GREAT SWITCH

As I mentioned in the introduction, the abortion business in the United States is declining. The trend is clear enough to receive media coverage. *Time* ran a cover story as early as May 4, 1992, which said, "While there are about 2,500 places around the country that provide abortions—down from a high of 2,908 ten years ago—they are mostly clustered around cities, leaving broad areas of the country unserved." The decline in clinics and doctors offering abortion has become all the more steep since then, with the number of clinics now being only in the hundreds.

The New York Times suggested in an editorial on October 13, 1994, that as abortion providers get scarcer, they also tend to be seedier. Young doctors see that doctors who perform abortions get little respect. Nor is it comforting to be one of a few, as the numbers dwindle. The *Times* dealt with the subject of dwindling abortion doctors in a lead article of thirteen pages on January 18, 1998.

Two days earlier to that, *ABC News* had a twenty-fifth-anniversary report on the *Roe v. Wade* Supreme Court decision and reported that 60 percent of doctors performing abortions are sixty-five or older. As more of them near retirement time, new doctors are entering the field in low numbers. Without an infusion of new providers, attrition alone will deal a deathly blow to the abortion business.

What followed the report is an important dynamic. After establishing this point, *ABC News* followed with a report on new medical advances in imaging the fetus. Peter Jennings commented that these were causing many to rethink abortion. Then came a report on efforts of the Catholic Church in postabortion healing in Project Rachel.

Positive reporting of pro-life views is infrequent. Yet there is a sound psychological principle explaining why these followed the report of precipitous decline in abortion doctors. It is the well-established theory of how "cognitive dissonance" makes people behave—how we all have a drive for consistency between our beliefs and feelings and behavior. If these elements are inconsistent, we feel tense. We try to relieve that tension by making them be consistent. When we see our behavior has changed, we look for reasons to account for the change.

In the Montgomery Bus Boycott, business leaders eventually found it in their best business interests to allow the racial integration being demanded. A cynic could say this was due to greed, not a change of heart. Greed may have been what changed the behavior, as it overrode racial prejudice. Once the behavior changed, however, so did the racial prejudice. When people noticed they were behaving differently, they accounted for it by an attitude consistent with the behavior. The social change in behavior was therefore made more permanent.[3]

In the 1970s and 1980s, these were two common ideas:

(1) The abortion business was expanding, with more and more clinics. The numbers climbed or maintained at a very high rate
(2) We are a noble and virtuous people

The first was a fact, making it more resistant to change. It can be unknown or ignored but not made untrue.

Yet the second point involved self-respect, again making it more resistant to change. Many pro-lifers decided it was not true (also a common attitude among peace activists). The public in general would be considerably less willing to drop it.

If both elements resisted change, then dealing with tension meant deciding they did not conflict with each other. The abortion-defending position became accepted not by reasoned argument, but because it resolved the tension between these two points by keeping them from looking like they disagree.

Any attack on the first point then became an attack on the truthfulness of the second. Pro-lifers had not merely been decrying the morality of abortion. Within their denunciation of abortion was a denunciation of the goodwill of the population. The same thing applied to those who decried current wars, impending executions, or the sorry state of poverty or racism and other bigotries.

The most daunting obstacle for abortion opponents had been that as long as the first point was a fact, people must decide that either the second point was untrue or the two points agreed with each other. Trying to convince them that the points did not agree left them with no other alternative than to decide that the second point was untrue. That point involved self-respect, so people were unwilling to do this. Therefore, efforts to persuade them that the two points did not agree found a major obstacle.

An alternative was saying that because the second element was true, therefore, the first element would not endure. This was a rhetorical strategy of the late Governor Robert Casey. He frequently said the defeat of abortion was inevitable because it could never last among the American people. Yet this point was more easily made when the first element actually started a process of not enduring.

There is now an entirely new situation from the previous decades. Under current conditions, there are new cognitive elements:

1. Abortion numbers are declining, fewer doctors are willing to do them, and clinics are scarcer
2. We are a noble and virtuous people

Once the first element has changed, it becomes reasonable to suggest that the second element caused the first. At least, the second point, so important to collective self-esteem, is actually strengthened by saying it caused the change.

In the earlier decades, the dynamics of tension-reduction strategies for cognitive dissonance, with the crucial importance of self-respect, worked against the antiabortion position. But a great reversal is now underway. Under new facts, the same dynamic works in its favor.

A *Newsweek* article called "Virgin Cool" illustrates how this works:

> Abortion, never an easy alternative for anyone, is even more daunting when you're young. Back in the '70s—and even the '80s—any woman worth her *Ms.* subscription knew she could pass around the hat in her dorm and collect a few hundred bucks for an abortion. Access was rarely a problem: every big city and most college towns had a clinic or at least an abortion doctor, and if he wasn't Marcus Welby, well, at least he had an office.... The climate has chilled; even ardent pro-choicers don't treat "choice" so lightly.[4]

Note the phrase, "if he wasn't Marcus Welby, well, at least he had an office." As a sense of collapse proceeds, it will be more and more safe to admit such ideas. It will be psychologically safer to bring scandals to public attention.

This goes beyond making it easier to admit things. We need such admissions to help us explain our behavior.

Other possibilities for accounting for our behavior abound—for example, the new information on the possible link of abortion to breast cancer. People will be more open to hearing information on emotional aftermath. The injustice of the situations pushing women into abortion will also be noticed more.

This reasoning also applies to executions. We didn't have DNA earlier to discover how many innocents there were on death row. We also find studies showing that it does not deter murder as well as we thought it did, which is important since deterring crime was supposed to be one of its major functions. Because we learn this new information, we change.

This may be why the *ABC News* story on the decline in the number of abortion doctors was followed by fetal pictures and positive programs to help women with abortion aftermath. If the decline seems inevitable, the next thing is to account for why. People will also seek information on how to live with the new situation.

The accommodation of abortion never really brought relief to the tension felt. However, the collapse of the institution *does* bring relief. The "Great Switch" will be powerful, because people want it. They want to avoid despair. They want hope. Once it looks possible, once it looks safe to express the desire that it actually happen, it will be a powerful dynamic.

This is why this book's introduction began with what the peace movement, the death penalty abolition movement, and the pro-life movement have achieved. We could instead have focused on how terrible the situation is in all cases. Military expenses are phenomenal and causing economic strain, and several smaller wars are happening at any given time. Executions are still numerous in large countries like the United States and China. Abortions are still in the millions worldwide with strong pressures to legalize them in more places. Pressures for pushing euthanasia and assisted suicide can still be documented as quite strong, allowing for the murder of Terri Schiavo with politicians assailed for trying to prevent it. Anybody who wants to be depressed can find ample material.

But depression is not a call to action. It's a call to give up and go home.

One of the most important strategic steps for pro-life education is to stress the declining numbers. This heartens those who have been working hard for years. For the public, a "bandwagon effect" may help. Most particularly, however, it lets people know that it is psychologically *safe* to let down their guard. That makes it possible to hear other information. It even motivates them to hear information they deliberately ignored before.

When a decline in the behavior is emphasized, the meaning of pro-life and/or peace-oriented information changes. Instead of being a cause for great tension, for alarm, for despair, for guilt, the same information accounts for the decline. Explaining what is wrong with any given practice of violence is converted from an undesirable encroachment on the mind to a desirable explanation of a positive turn of events.

I used this psychological dynamic to start this book with positive, true information on how successful movements against violence have recently been. My experience says that some readers would have kept reading because of that, who would have put the book down in disgust had I started off explaining how terrible our situation is.

We've come full circle now—using the behavior of consistency to help advance the cause of consistency of behavior.

NOTES AND REFERENCES

1. Follett, Mary Parker. 1940. Constructive Conflict. In H. C. Metcalf and L. Urwick, eds., *Dynamic Administration: The Collected Papers of Mary Parker Follett*. New York: Harper.

2. Borger, Gloria. April 11, 2005. A Time for Uncertainty. *U.S. News and World Report*, 34.

3. Pelton, Leroy H. 1974. *The Psychology of Nonviolence*. New York: Pergamon.

4. Ingrassia, Michele. October 17, 1994. Virgin Cool. *Newsweek*, p. 60.

About the Editors and Contributors

RACHEL M. MACNAIR is Director of the Institute for Integrated Social Analysis, research arm of Consistent Life. She is also author of *Psychology of Peace: An Introduction* (Praeger, 2003) and *Perpetration Induced Traumatic Stress: The Psychological Consequences of Killing* (Praeger, 2002).

STEPHEN ZUNES is a professor of politics and international studies at the University of San Francisco, where he chairs the Middle East studies program. He serves as a member of the advisory committee for the Tikkun Community and as the chair of the board of academic advisors for the International Center on Nonviolent Conflict. Previous books include *Tinderbox: U.S. Middle East Policy and the Roots of Terrorism* (Common Courage Press, 2003) and *Nonviolent Social Movements: A Geographical Perspective* (Blackwell Publishers, 1999).

EDITH BOGUE is Assistant Professor of Sociology at the College of Saint Scholastica in Duluth, Minnesota. She is a monastic in the Order of St. Benedict.

WILLIAM BRENNAN is Professor of Social Work in the Saint Louis University School of Social Work. He wrote *Dehumanizing the Vulnerable: When Word Games Take Lives* (Loyola University Press, 1995) and is working on a book tentatively entitled *Killing in the Name of Healing: Technology, Rhetoric, and the Medicalization of Destruction.*

CAROL CROSSED has served as Executive Director of Consistent Life when it was named the Seamless Garment Network and has served as President of Democrats for Life of America.

MARY KRANE DERR edits the Nonviolent Choice Directory (www.nonviolentchoice.info). She read her poetry at the 1999 Parliament of the World's Religions, Cape Town, South Africa, and coedited the book *ProLife Feminism: Yesterday and Today* (Xlibris, 2006).

NAT HENTOFF has written over 25 books, including history, novels, and a special concern for free speech rights. He is a columnist for the *Village Voice, The Progressive, JazzTimes, Legal Times, Free Inquiry, Jewish World Review,* and others.

JAMES R. KELLY is Professor of Sociology at Fordham University in Bronx, New York.

MARY MEEHAN is a writer and public speaker from Cumberland, Maryland, and editor of Meehan Reports (www.meehanreports.com).

VASU MURTI was born and raised in Southern California in a family of South Indian Brahmins. He holds degrees in physics and applied mathematics from the University of California. He is author of *The Liberal Case Against Abortion* (Rage Media, 2007).

MICHAEL N. NAGLER is Professor Emeritus of Classics and Comparative Literature at the University of California at Berkeley, where he founded the Peace and Conflict Studies Program. He is President of the board of METTA: Center for Nonviolence Education, and cofounded Educators for Nonviolence. He is the author of *Is There No Other Way? The Search for a Nonviolent Future* (Berkeley Hill Books, 2001).

THOMAS W. STRAHAN was an attorney who compiled as a reference book the bibliography called *Detrimental Effects of Abortion: An Annotated Bibliography with Commentary* (Acorn Books, 2001).

Index